# The Story of
# The Guides

The Exploits of the Soldiers of the Famous Indian Army Regiment from the Northwest Frontier 1847 – 1900

## G. J. Younghusband

*The Story of the Guides: The Exploits of the Soldiers of the Famous Indian Army Regiment from the Northwest Frontier 1847 - 1900*
by G. J. Younghusband

Published by Leonaur Ltd

Copyright in this form © 2006 Leonaur Ltd

ISBN (10 digit): 1-84677-073-4 (hardcover)
ISBN (13 digit): 978-1-84677-073-9 (hardcover)

ISBN (10 digit): 1-84677-063-7 (softcover)
ISBN (13 digit): 978-1-84677-063-0 (softcover)

http://www.leonaur.com

**Publisher's Notes**

In the interests of authenticity, the spellings, grammar and place names used have been retained from the original editions.

The opinions of the authors represent a view of events in which he was a participant related from his own perspective, as such the text is relevant as an historical document.

The views expressed in this book are not necessarily those of the publisher.

# Contents

First Steps in War ................................................................ 9
The Fighting Round Mooltan & After ........................24
The Capture of the Fort of Gorindghar ......................36
On the Frontier in the 'Fifties .........................................42
The Story of Dilawur Khan .............................................53
The Great March to Delhi ...............................................64
Twenty Years of Minor Wars ...........................................74
The Massacre of the Guides at Kabul, 1879 ....................94
The Afghan War, 1878 - 1880 ........................................113
War Stories ......................................................................129
Adventures of Shah Sowar & Abdul Mujid ................138
The Relief of Chitral .......................................................152
The Malakand, 1897 .......................................................163
The Home of the Guides ................................................175

From the Leonaur book
## Tommy Atkins War Stories

Recollectionsof the Indian Mutiny
by Gunner McCallum, Royal Artillery ........................193

# Photographs & Illustrations

Sir Harry Lumsden, who raised the Guides, from a portrait made when he was commanding the corps *frontispiece*

Afridis on the war-path *p. 15*

Ressaldar Fatteh Khan, Khuttuk, who at the head of seventy men of the Guides' Cavalry defeated and drove into Mooltan a Brigade of Sikh Cavalry, from a picture by W. Carpenter *p. 29*

A Picquet of the Guides' Infantry bivouacking *p. 43*

A Scout of the Guides' Cavalry warning his Infantry Comrades. The small man on the right is a Gurkha *p. 69*

A non-commissioned officer of the Guides' Infantry *p. 77*

An Afridi of the Guides' Infantry *p. 89*

The Memorial Arch and Tank to the memory of Sir Louis Cavignari and the officers and non-commissioned officers and men of the Guides killed in the defence of the Kabul Residency, September 3, 1879 *p. 99*

Statue of Lieutenant Walter Hamilton, erected in Dublin Museum *p. 103*

A Trooper of the Guides' Cavalry *p. 117*

Types of men in the Guides' Infantry *p. 131*

Types of men in the Guides' Cavalry, both in uniform and mufti *p. 139*

Non-commissioned Officer and Trooper of the Guides' Cavalry *p. 155*

Thirty-four wearers of the Star For Valour, all serving at one time in the Corps of Guides. This is the highest distinction open to an Indian soldier for gallantry in action. *p. 165*

The old Graveyard at Mardan *p. 179*

The Church at Mardan *p. 185*

# Chapter 1
# First Steps in War

It is given to some regiments to spread their achievements over the quiet centuries, while to the lot of others it falls to live, for a generation or two, in an atmosphere of warlike strife and ever present danger. The Guides have been, from a soldier's point of view, somewhat fortunate in seeing much service during the past sixty years, and thus their history lends itself readily to a narrative which is full of adventure and stirring deeds. The story of those deeds may, perchance, be found of interest to those at home, who like to read the gallant record of the men who fight their battles in remote and unfamiliar corners of the Empire across the seas.

To Sir Henry Lawrence, the *preux chevalier,* who died a soldier's death in the hallowed precincts of Lucknow, the Guides owe their name and origin. At a time when soldiers fought, and marched, and lived in tight scarlet tunics, high stocks, trousers tightly strapped over Wellington boots, and shakos which would now be looked on as certain death, Sir Henry evolved the startling heresy that to get the best work out of troops, and to enable them to undertake great exertions, it was necessary that the soldier should be loosely, comfortably, and suitably clad, that something more substantial than a pill-box with a pocket-handkerchief wrapped round it was required as a protection from a tropical sun, and that footgear must be made for marching, and not for parading round a band-stand.

Martinets of the old school gravely shook their heads,

and trembled for the discipline of men without stocks and overalls. Men of the Irregular Cavalry, almost as much trussed and padded as their Regular comrades (who were often so tightly clad as to be unable to mount without assistance), looked with good-natured tolerance on a foredoomed failure. But Sir Henry Lawrence had the courage of his opinions, and determined to put his theories to practice, though at first on a small scale.

Not only were the Guides to be sensibly clothed, but professionally also they were to mark a new departure. In 1846 the Punjab was still a Sikh province, and the administration was only thinly strengthened by a sprinkling of British officers. Men, half soldiers, half civilians, and known in India under the curious misnomer of Political Officers,--a class to whom the British Empire owes an overwhelming debt--were scattered here and there, hundreds of miles apart, and in the name of the Sikh Durbar practically ruled and administered provinces as large as Ireland or Scotland. The only British troops in the country were a few of the Company's regiments, quartered at Lahore to support the authority of the Resident,--a mere coral island in the wide expanse. What Sir Henry Lawrence felt was the want of a thoroughly mobile body of troops, both horse and foot, untrammelled by tradition, ready to move at a moment's notice, and composed of men of undoubted loyalty and devotion, troops who would not only be of value in the rough and tumble of a soldier's trade, but would grow used to the finer arts of providing skilled intelligence.

The title selected for the corps was in itself a new departure in the British Army, and history is not clear as to whether its pre-ordained duties suggested the designation to Sir Henry Lawrence, or whether, in some back memory, its distinguished predecessor in the French army stood sponsor for the idea. Readers of the Napoleonic wars will remember that, after the battle of Borghetto, the Great

Captain raised a *Corps des Guides*, and that this was the first inception of the *Corps d'Elite*, which later grew into the Consular Guard, and later still expanded into the world-famed Imperial Guard ten thousand strong.

But whatever the history of the inception of its title, the duties of the Corps of Guides were clearly and concisely defined in accordance with Sir Henry's precepts. It was to contain trustworthy men, who could, at a moment's notice, act as guides to troops in the field; men capable, too, of collecting trustworthy intelligence beyond, as well as within, our borders; and, in addition to all this, men, ready to give and take hard blows, whether on the frontier or in a wider field. A special rate of pay was accorded to all ranks. And finally, fortunate as Sir Henry Lawrence had been in the inspiration that led him to advocate this new departure, he was no less fortunate in his selection of the officer who was destined to inaugurate a new feature in the fighting forces of the Empire.

Even from among officers of proved experience and ability it is by no means easy to select the right man to inaugurate and carry through successfully an experimental measure; much more difficult is it to do so when the selection lies among young officers who have still to win their spurs. Yet from among old or young, experienced or inexperienced, it would have been impossible to have selected an officer with higher qualifications for the work in hand than the young man on whom the choice fell.

Born of a soldier stock, and already experienced in war, Harry Lumsden possessed all the finest attributes of the young British officer. He was a man of strong character, athletic, brave, resolute, cool and resourceful in emergency; a man of rare ability and natural aptitude for war, and possessed, moreover, of that magnetic influence which communicates the highest confidence and devotion to those who follow. In addition he was a genial comrade, a keen sportsman, and a rare friend to all who knew him. Such, then, was the young officer selected by Sir Henry Lawrence to raise the Corps of Guides.

That the commencement should be not too ambitious, it was ruled that the first nucleus should consist only of one troop of cavalry and two companies of infantry, with only one British officer. But as this story will show, as time and success hallowed its standards, this modest squad expanded into the corps which now, with twenty-seven British officers and fourteen hundred men, holds an honoured place in the ranks of the Indian Army.

Following out the principle that the corps was to be for service and not for show, the time-honoured scarlet of the British Army was laid aside for the dust-coloured uniform which half a century later, under the now well-known name of khaki, became the fighting dress of the whole of the land forces of the Empire.

The spot chosen for raising the new corps was Peshawur, then the extreme outpost of the British position in India, situated in the land of men born and bred to the fighting trade, free-lances ready to take service wherever the rewards and spoils of war were to be secured. While fully appreciating the benefits of accurate drill, and the minute attention to technical detail, bequeathed as a legacy by the school of Wellington, Lumsden upheld the principle that the greatest and best school for war is war itself. He believed in the elasticity which begets individual self-confidence, and preferred a body of men taught to act and fight with personal intelligence to the highly-trained impersonality which requires a sergeant's order before performing the smallest duty, and an officer's fostering care to forestall its every need.

Holding such views, it is with no surprise we read that, while his men were still under the elementary training of drill instructors borrowed from other regiments, Lumsden led them forth to learn the art of war under the blunt and rugged conditions of the Indian frontier. To march, not through peaceful lanes, but with all the care and precautions which a semi-hostile region necessitated; to encamp, not on the quiet village green where sentry-go might appear an unmeaning farce, but in close contact with a vigilant and active race of hard fighters, especially skilled in the arts of surprises and night-attacks; to be ready, always ready, with the readiness of those who meet difficulties half way,--such were the precepts which the hardy recruits of the Guides imbibed simultaneously with the automatic instruction of the drill-sergeant.

Nor was it long before Lumsden had an opportunity of practically demonstrating to the young idea his methods of making war. The corps, barely seven months old, was encamped at Kàlu Khan in the plain of Yusafzai, when sudden orders came, directing it to make a night-march, with the object of surprising and capturing the village of Mughdara in the Panjtar Hills. In support of the small band of Guides was sent a troop of Sikh cavalry, seasoned warriors, to stiffen the young endeavour and hearten the infant warrior. Marching all night, half an hour before daylight the force arrived at the mouth of a narrow defile, three-fourths of a mile long, leading to the village, and along which only one horseman could advance at a time. Nothing dismayed, and led by the intrepid Lumsden, in single file the Guides dashed at full gallop through the defile, fell with fury on the awakening village, captured and disarmed it, and brought away, as trophies of war, its chief and three hundred head of cattle. To add to the modest pride taken in this bright initial feat of arms, it was achieved single-handed, for the supporting troop of Sikhs failed to face the dark terrors of the defile and remained behind. This opening skirmish was the keynote to many an after success. It helped to foster a spirit of alert preparedness, readiness to seize the fleeting opportunity, and courage and determination when once committed to action. These seeds thus planted grew to be some of the acknowledged attributes of the force as it blossomed into maturity under its gallant leader.

During the first year of its existence the young corps was engaged in several more of the same class of enterprise, and in all acquitted itself with quiet distinction. As, however, the history of one is in most particulars that of another, it will not be necessary to enter into a detailed account of each.

The British in the Peshawur Valley, as elsewhere in the Punjab, were in a somewhat peculiar position. They were not administering, or policing, the country on behalf of the British Government, but in the name of the Sikh Durbar. In the Peshawur Valley, in which broad term may be included the plains of Yusafzai, the Sikh rule was but feebly maintained amidst a warlike race of an antagonistic faith. In the matter of the collection of revenue, therefore, the ordinary machinery of government was not sufficiently strong to effect regular and punctual payment; and consequently, when any village or district was much in arrears, it became customary to send a body of troops to collect the revenue. If the case was merely one of dilatoriness, unaccompanied by hostile intent, the case was sufficiently met by the payment of the arrears due, and by bearing the cost of feeding the troops while the money was being collected. But more often, dealing as they were with a weak and discredited government, the hardy warriors of the frontier, sending their wives and cattle to some safe glen in the distant hills, openly defied both the tax-collector and the troops that followed him. It then became a case either of coercion or of leaving it alone.

An effete administration, like that of the Sikhs, if thus roughly faced, as often as not let the matter rest. But with the infusion of British blood a new era commenced; and the principle was insisted on that, where revenue was due,

Afridis on the war-path

the villagers must pay or fight. And further, if they chose the latter alternative, a heavy extra penalty would fall on them, such as the confiscation of their cattle, the destruction of their strongholds, and the losses inevitable when the appeal is made to warlike arbitration.

It was on such an expedition that one of the Guides had a curious and fatal adventure. Colonel George Lawrence, who was the British Representative in Peshawur, was out in Yusafzai with a brigade of Sikh troops, collecting revenue and generally asserting the rights of government. Co-operating with him was Lumsden with the Guides. Among the recalcitrants was the village of Babuzai, situated in a strong position in the Lundkwar Valley, and Lawrence determined promptly to coerce it. His plan of operation was to send the Guides' infantry by night to work along the hills, so that before daylight they would be occupying the commanding heights behind the village, and thus cut off escape into the mountains. He himself, at dawn, would be in position with the Sikh brigade to attack from the open plain; while the Guides' cavalry were disposed so as to cut off the retreat to the right up the valley.

In pursuance of their portion of the plan of operations, as the Guides' infantry were cautiously moving along the hills towards their allotted position, in the growing light they suddenly came upon a picquet of the enemy placed to guard against this very contingency. To fire was to give the alarm, so with exceeding promptness the picquet was charged with the bayonet, and overpowered. At the head of the small storming party charged a duffadar[1] of the Guides' cavalry, by name Fatteh Khan. Fatteh Khan was one of those men to whom it was as the breath of life to be in every brawl and fight within a reasonable ride. On

---

1. Duffadar, a native non-commissioned officer of cavalry, answering to the naik (corporal) of infantry.

this occasion he was of opinion that the cavalry would see little or no fighting, whereas the infantry might well be in for a pretty piece of hand-to-hand work. "To what purpose therefore, Sahib, should I waste my day?" he said to Lumsden. "With your Honour's permission I will accompany my infantry comrades on foot. Are we not all of one corps?" And so he went, keeping well forward, and handy for the first encounter.

As the gallant duffadar, sword in hand, dashed at the picquet, he was from a side position shot through both arms; but not a whit dismayed or hindered he hurled himself with splendid courage at the most brawny opponent he could single out. A short sharp conflict ensued, Fatteh Khan with his disabled arm using his sword, while his opponent, with an Affghan knife in one hand, was busy trying to induce the glow on his matchlock to brighten up, that the gun might definitely settle the issue. In the course of the skirmishing between the two men a curious accident, however, occurred. The tribesman, as was usual in those days, was carrying under his arm a goat-skin bag full of powder for future use. In aiming a blow at him, Fatteh Khan missed his man, but cut a hole in the bag; the powder began to run out, and, as ill chance would have it, some fell on the glowing ember of the matchlock. This weapon, pointed anywhere and anyhow at the moment, went off with a terrific report, which was followed instantaneously by a still greater explosion. The flame had caught the bag of powder, and both the gallant duffadar and his staunch opponent were blown to pieces.

So died a brave soldier. But lest the noise should have betrayed them, his comrades hurried on with increased eagerness, and as good fortune would have it arrived in position at the very nick of time. The operation was completely successful. In due course the Sikhs attacked in front, and when the enemy tried to escape up the hills behind their village, they found retreat cut off by the Guides' infantry. Turning back, they essayed to break away to the right; but the intention being signalled to the Guides' cavalry, who were placed so as to intercept the fugitives, these fell with great vigour on the tribesmen and gave them a much needed lesson. It was now no longer an effete Sikh administration that breakers of the law had to deal with, but the strong right arm and warlike guile of the British officer, backed up by men who meant fighting.

\* \* \* \* \*

It was now the spring of 1848, and great events were brewing in the Punjab. It was the lull between the two stormy gusts of the First and Second Sikh Wars. To us at this date it does not seem to require the omniscience of a prophet, prophesying after the event, to discover that the settlement arrived at after the First Sikh War contained most of the possible elements of an unpermanent nature.

The Punjab was to remain a Sikh province, with the infant son of the Lion of the Punjab as its Sovereign; but the real ruler of the kingdom of the Sikhs was a British officer, Henry Lawrence, at the head of a council of regency. To support his authority British bayonets overawed the capital of the Punjab, and assumed the mien of those who hold their place by right of conquest. Attached to, but really at the head of, the minor centres of administration, were men like Herbert Edwardes, Abbott, Taylor, George Lawrence, Nicholson, and Agnew; the stamp of high-souled pioneer who though alone, unguarded, and hundreds of miles from succour, by sheer force of character makes felt the weight of British influence in favour of just and cleanly government. And acting thus honourably they were naturally detested by the lower class of venal rulers, whose idea of government was, and is at all times and on all occasions, by persuasion, force, or oppression, to squeeze dry the people committed to their charge. Ready to the hand of a discontented satrap, sighing for the illicit gains of a less austere rule, were the bands of discharged soldiers, their occupation gone, who crowded every village. It was easy to show, as was indeed the case, that these discontented warriors owed their present plight to the hated English. For while one of the conditions of peace, after the First Sikh War, insisted on the disbandment of the greater portion of the formidable Sikh army, the enlightened expedient of enlisting our late enemies into our own army had not yet been acted upon to any great extent. To add to the danger, every town and hamlet harboured the chiefs and people of only a half-lost cause.

Thus the train of revolt was laid with an almost fatal precision throughout the province, and only required the smallest spark to set it alight. At the head of the incendiary movement was the Maharani, the wife of the late and mother of the present infant king. Some inkling of the plot, as could hardly fail, came to the British Resident's ears, the primary step contemplated being to seduce from their allegiance the Company's troops quartered at Lahore.

It was at this stage that a summons reached Lumsden to march with all despatch to Lahore, a distance of two hundred and fifty miles. Here was an opportunity of testing the value of a corps whose loyalty was above question, and which from its composition could have no sympathy with the movement. Consequently to Lumsden and his men was assigned the difficult and unaccustomed duty of unravelling the plot and bringing the conspirators to justice. Setting to work with his accustomed readiness, and aided by one of his ressaldars,[2] Fatteh Khan, Khuttuk, of whose prowess on many a bloody field the story will in due course be told, Lumsden with characteris-

---

2. Ressaldar, a native commissioned officer of cavalry.

tic alacrity undertook this intricate and dangerous duty. His tracks covered, so to speak, by the unsuspicious bearing of a blunt soldier in command of a corps of rugged trans-border warriors, the unaccustomed rôle of a skilled detective was carried out with promptness and success. In the course of a very few days some of the Guides had obtained conclusive proof regarding three matters: that the Maharani was at the head of the movement, that her chief agent was the Sikh general Khan Singh, and that the Company's troops had already been tampered with.

As the plot thickened it was discovered that a meeting of the conspirators, including fifty or sixty men of various regiments, was to take place on a certain night at a certain place. Lumsden patiently awaited the event, intending with the Guides to surround and capture the conspirators red-handed. But, on the night fixed for the meeting, a retainer of General Khan Singh came to visit one of the Guides, with whom he was on friendly terms, and in the course of conversation made it evident that his master was not easy in his mind, why not no one could say, and that he had half determined on flight. The man of the Guides, leaving his friend in charge of a comrade, with commendable acumen hastened to Lumsden and told him the story. That officer at once saw that the moment had come to strike, lest the prey escape. He therefore immediately clapped the Sikh general's retainer into the quarterguard, much to that individual's astonishment, and promptly parading the Guides, hurried down to the city and surrounded Khan Singh's house.

It was now past eleven o'clock, the house was in darkness and strongly barricaded all round; the city was that of a foreign power, and no police, or other, warrant did Lumsden hold. But he was no man to stand on ceremony, or shirk responsibility, nor was he one for a moment to count on the personal risks he ran. Finding the doors stouter than they expected, his men burst in a window, and headed by their intrepid officer dashed into the building. There, overcoming promptly any show of resistance, they seized General Khan Singh, his munshi[3] and a confidential agent, together with a box of papers, and under close guard carried them back to the Guides' camp. In due course the prisoners were tried and conclusive evidence being furnished, and confirmed by the incriminating documents found in the box, General Khan Singh and his munshi were sentenced to be hanged. This prompt dealing served at once to check rebellion in the vicinity of Lahore, and placed the Company's troops beyond the schemes of conspirators.

Amongst other papers found in Khan Singh's box were some which clearly inculpated the Maharani, and it was at once decided to deport her beyond the region of effective intrigue. The lady was, under arrangements made for her by the Government, at this time residing in one of the late Maharaja's palaces at Sheikapura about twenty-three miles from Lahore. To Lumsden and his men was entrusted the duty of arresting and deporting the firebrand princess. As taking part in this mission, first appears in the annals of the Guides the name of Lieutenant W.S.R. Hodson, afterwards famous for his many deeds of daring, and whose name still lives as the intrepid and dashing leader of Hodson's Horse. Appointed as adjutant and second-in-command to a born exponent of sound, yet daring, methods of warfare, his early training in the Guides stood him in good stead in his brief, stirring, and glorious career.

In the execution of their orders Lumsden and Hodson with the Guides' cavalry set off quietly after dark for their twenty-three miles ride. The service was of some difficulty and of no little danger, for not only might the Maharani's numerous partisans make an armed resistance, but failing

---

3. Munshi, a secretary or clerk.

this they might organise a formidable rescue party to cut off the enterprise between Sheikapura and the Ravi. Against any such attempt, made with resources well within hail, the slender troop of the Guides would naturally come in for some rough buffeting. Much, however, to the surprise, and possibly the relief, of the British officers, they were received not only without any signs of hostility, but with smiles of well-assumed welcome. The explanation of this was that somehow news of the fate of General Khan Singh had already reached the Maharani, and with Eastern diplomacy she was preparing to trim her bark on the other tack. Even to the suggestion that she should prepare to make a journey she raised no objection; and it was only when she found herself on the road to Ferozepore, and learnt that her destination was Benares, that the courtesy and dignity of a queen gave place to torrents of scurrilous abuse and invective such as the dialects of India are pre-eminently capable of supplying.

## Chapter 2
# The Fighting Round Mooltan & After

These prompt measures, however, served only a local and temporary purpose, effective but little beyond striking distance of the troops stationed at Lahore. The flame of unrest damped down here had burst forth under a different banner at Mooltan, where the Diwan Mulraj farmed the province under treaty with the Sikhs. The Diwan himself was a miserable personality, but carried away by the tide of popular feeling, he became inextricably involved in antagonism to the British cause by the cold-blooded murder of Agnew and Anderson. These two British officers, with the full consent and support of the Sikh Durbar, had been sent to Mooltan on special duty in connection with the voluntary abdication of Mulraj, which had been accepted by his suzeraine. The escort sent with the British officers was a strong one, and, if loyal, perfectly competent to deal with any disorders. It consisted of fourteen hundred Sikhs, a regiment of Gurkhas, seven hundred cavalry, and six guns.

This seemingly formidable and carefully composed body of troops proved, however, to be entirely unreliable. Agnew and Anderson were, within a few hours of their arrival at Mooltan, attacked and severely wounded by fanatics, and no one raised a hand to help them. Lying helpless and sorely wounded in the temporary asylum which their quarters afforded, they heard with dismay that practically the whole of the escort on whom their safety depended had gone over to the faction of Mulraj, a faction which insisted on his remaining in power, and which was strongly antagonistic to the claims of British political influence. Alone amid thousands, it remained only for these brave young officers to offer up their lives on the altar of British dominion.

Thus strongly committed to a line of action which was far from according with his weak and vacillating nature, Mulraj raised the standard of revolt, and sending the fiery cross through the country, called on all to join in expelling the hated foreigner, and common enemy, from the Land of the Five Rivers. The prospects of the cause looked bright indeed. No organised body of British troops lay nearer than Lahore, hundreds of miles distant; the hot season had commenced, when the movement of regular troops encounters almost insuperable difficulties; the whole country was smarting under the sense of recent severe but hardly conclusive defeat; while hundreds of petty chiefs, and thousands of soldiers, were chafing under the thinly disguised veil of foreign sovereignty.

Yet out of the unlooked for West arose a star which in a few brief weeks eclipsed the rising moon of national aspiration, and, shining bright and true, helped to guide the frail bark of British supremacy through victory to the haven of a permanent peace. That star was an unknown British subaltern named Herbert Edwardes. Edwardes was one of the young officers deputed to assist the Sikhs in the work of systemising and purifying their administration, and was at this time engaged in the revenue settlement of the Dera-Ismail-Khan district. One day in June as he sat in court settling disputes, there came to him a runner, covered with dust and sweat, who brought to him a last message from Agnew, as he lay wounded on his bed in Mooltan. The message asked urgently for help, and appealed, as the writer knew, to one who would spare no risk or pains to furnish it. To succour the wounded British officers was a matter which had passed beyond the region of possibility, for the ink had hardly dried on their message before they were murdered; but to re-establish the prestige of the British name, to reassert its dignity and influence, and to bring to punishment the perpetrators of a hideous and treacherous crime,--these tasks Herbert Edwardes at once set before himself.

Alone, save for the presence of one other Englishman, the young British subaltern, with the sage intrepidity of ripest experience, hastily summoned the chiefs of the Derajat and Bannu districts to his aid, and assembled their motley followings under his banner. He sent messengers to the friendly chief of Bhawulpore, and called on him to join in the crusade against Mooltan. Then after much feinting and fencing, and greatly assisted by the stout Van Cortlandt, Edwardes threw his army across the Indus, at this season a roaring torrent three miles wide, and sought out his enemy. Coming up with him he defeated Mulraj and his army of ten thousand men in two pitched battles, and drove him to take refuge behind the walls of Mooltan.

Accompanying Herbert Edwardes was a detachment of the Guides, lent by Lumsden, and before the war bent on learning their way about this portion of the frontier, in accordance with the rôle assigned their corps. This detachment not only joined with natural zest in the hard fighting that fell to the share of all, but proved of great service to the commander as scouts and intelligence men. So far did intrepidity and love of adventure carry them, that four sowars,[4] under Duffadar Khanan Khan, rode through the enemy's outposts, and with admirable coolness picketed their horses, probably without excessive ostentation, amidst the enemy's cavalry. They then separated, and went about to see and remember that which might be useful to their own commander and their own comrades in the war. It is perhaps needless to say that discovery meant instant death, yet, with the happy insolence of the born free-lance, superb

---

4. Sowar, a native trooper.

indifference carried them through where the slightest slip would have been fatal. Indeed, one of them, by name Mohaindin, with nerves of steel, actually succeeded in being taken on as an orderly by Diwan Mulraj himself, and while acting as such was severely wounded by a round shot from one of our own guns at the battle of Sadusam.

Meanwhile the headquarters of the Guides, under Lumsden, were hastening down from Lahore to give Edwardes that invaluable support which, however meagre in numbers, stout hearts, whose loyalty is above suspicion, afford to a harassed commander. Joyfully were they welcomed, as one sweltering day in June the Guides joined the little force which was besieging an army of equal or perhaps greater strength lying behind the growing ramparts of Mooltan.

Nor were the new arrivals long in showing their mettle. The camp was then pitched on the right of the nullah at Suraj Kund, and in this position was much annoyed by twelve pieces of ordnance, placed in position round the Bibi Pakdaman mosque. These Lumsden offered to capture and silence and, if possible, bring away. The service was carried out with much dash and gallantry, and the guns were captured and rendered useless, though it was found impossible, in face of the heavy odds, to bring them off.

But the siege of Mooltan, in so far as the Guides were concerned, was chiefly memorable for bringing prominently to notice the gallant and romantic figure of Fatteh Khan, Khuttuk. This noble fellow was one of those Bayards of the East who know no fear, and as soldiers are without reproach. Born of a fighting stock and fighting tribe, cradled amidst wars and alarms, he developed the highest qualities of a brave, resolute, and resourceful partisan leader. Always ready, always alert, nothing could upset his equanimity, nothing take him by surprise, while no odds were too great for him to face. With the true instinct of the cavalry leader he struck hard and promptly, and upheld in person the doctrine that boldness, even unto recklessness, should be the watchword of the light cavalryman. Yet this paladin of the fight could barely write his name. It is not every soldier who has the opportunity nowadays, as in the days of champions, to perform a historic deed in the open with both armies as spectators. Yet so it happened to Ressaldar Fatteh Khan one hot day in August, 1848, before the walls of Mooltan.

Lumsden was absent on some duty; indeed, there were only three British officers, and these took turn and turn about in the trenches, when a messenger galloped into the Guides' camp to report that a marauding party of the enemy's cavalry, some twenty strong, had driven off a herd of General Whish's camels which were grazing near his camp. Fatteh Khan, as ressaldar, was the senior officer in camp, and at once gave the order for every man to boot and saddle and get to horse at once. The little party, numbering barely seventy, led by Fatteh Khan, followed the messenger at a gallop for three miles to the scene of the raid. Arrived there they suddenly found themselves confronted, not by a marauding troop of horsemen hastily driving off a herd of camels, but by the whole force of the enemy's cavalry, some twelve hundred strong. These veteran swordsmen and lancers, of whose skill and bravery in battle we had had ample proof during this and previous wars, had been sent out to intercept a convoy of treasure expected in the British camp. Having, however, failed in their mission, they were leisurely returning to Mooltan, when a little cloud appeared on their fighting horizon. Some returning patrol, no doubt, they thought, some frightened stragglers driven in perhaps, some stampeding mules or ponies. But no! the little cloud now discloses a little line of horsemen, tearing along as if the devil drove. The whole mass of cavalry, like startled deer, halted and stared at this reckless onslaught; and while thus

RESSALDAR FATTEH KHAN, KHUTTUK, WHO AT THE HEAD OF SEVENTY MEN OF THE GUIDES' CAVALRY DEFEATED AND DROVE INTO MOOLTAN A BRIGADE OF SIKH CAVALRY, FROM A PICTURE BY W. CARPENTER

standing, transfixed with astonishment, Fatteh Khan and his gallant troop of Guides were on them.

Yelling fiercely, with lance and sword the Guides clove their way through the huddling mass of the enemy. Then clearing, they wheeled about, and with unabated fury fell again upon the benumbed and paralysed foe. Not yet content, the heroic Khuttuk again called on his men for another effort, and, rallying and wheeling about, the weary troopers and still wearier horses once more rode down into the stricken mass. But "God preserve us from these fiends," muttered the demoralised Sikhs, and, assisting their deity to answer the pious prayer, the whole mass broke and fled, pursued up to the very walls of Mooltan by "that thrice accursed son of perdition, Fatteh Khan, Khuttuk," and the remnants of his seventy Guides.

Through the intense heat of the summer of 1848 the little cluster of English officers who stood for British dominion kept heart and energy in the siege of Mooltan. As Edwardes described the position, it was only a terrier watching a tiger; but it was at any rate a good stout-hearted English terrier, and the tiger was afraid to face it. Yet even this stout terrier had to give way a little, when no reinforcements arrived, and when, in September, Sher Sing, with three thousand four hundred cavalry and nine hundred infantry, deserted and went over to the enemy.

The siege, however, was only temporarily raised, and was at once resumed on the arrival of a column of Bombay troops. This reinforcement consisted of two British infantry regiments, five Native infantry regiments, and three regiments of Native cavalry. With his force thus strengthened General Whish immediately resumed the offensive, and not only renewed the siege, but determined to take the place by assault. In the furtherance of this project he first stormed and captured the city, many of the buildings in which completely dominated the fort at short effective ranges. From the coigns of vantage thus gained the British artillery and infantry poured a hail of shot and shell into the doomed defences, while the cavalry hovered outside ready to pounce on those who broke cover. Placed in these desperate straits, and without hope of succour, Diwan Mulraj and the whole of his force surrendered unconditionally on the 22nd of January, 1849, after a siege which had lasted nearly seven months.

This timely success released at a critical moment, for service elsewhere, the British forces engaged in the siege. For meanwhile great events had been happening in the upper Punjab, and great were yet to come. On January 13th had been fought the bloody battle of Chillianwalla, where the casualties on both sides were very severe, and where the gallant 24th Foot had thirteen officers and the sergeant-major laid out dead on their mess-table. Lord Gough required nearly three thousand men to fill the gaps in his ranks before again closing with the redoubtable Sikhs. On every count, therefore, the news of the fall of Mooltan was received with considerable satisfaction, and the troops recently engaged in it with keen alacrity turned their faces northwards to Lord Gough's assistance, in the hope of arriving in time to throw their weight into the balance in the closing scenes of a campaign destined to add a kingdom to the British Empire.

Ahead of the troops from Mooltan went Lumsden and the Guides' cavalry, followed by Hodson with the Guides' infantry. The corps when re-united, before it joined Lord Gough, was deflected for the performance of a detached duty which brought it no little honour. It was reported that considerable numbers of Sikh troops, under Ganda Singh and Ram Singh, having crossed the Chenab, were moving south-east heavily laden with spoil, which having disposed of, they would be free to fall on the British lines of communication.

Starting in hot haste, Lumsden and Hodson took up the trail, and by dogged and relentless pursuit, after three days and nights of incessant marching, came up with their quarry. They found Ganda Singh and his following at Nuroat on the Beas River, while Ram Singh was some miles further on.

The position taken up by Ganda Singh was in a clump of mango trees, surrounded by a square ditch and bank in place of a hedge, as is often the case in the East. This formed a good natural defence, and piling their spoil up amongst the trees, Ganda Singh prepared to fight desperately to hold what they had won with so much toil. The right of the Sikh position rested on a deep and tortuous nullah, or dry watercourse, whose precipitous sides, if properly watched, formed an excellent flank defence; but if unwatched they formed an equally admirable covered approach whereby an opponent might penetrate or turn the position. The manifest precaution of setting a watch was, however, neglected, an error not likely to slip the attention of so skilled a campaigner as Lumsden. Occupying, therefore, the attention of the enemy in front by preparations for the infantry attack under Hodson, Lumsden himself, with the cavalry, slipped into the nullah, and working quietly past the enemy's flank emerged on to his rear at a spot where a friendly clump of sugar-cane afforded further concealment till the appointed moment. A signal was now made for Hodson to attack vigorously in front, which he accordingly did, and after severe fighting drove the enemy into the open. Seizing the auspicious moment, Lumsden issued from his shelter, and falling like a whirlwind on the retiring enemy, literally swept them from the face of the earth; one man only escaped to tell the tale. Amongst the recovered loot were found the silver kettle-drums of the 2nd Irregular Cavalry lost in the recent fighting, and amongst the slain was Ganda

Singh. General Wheler coming up on the following day, the combined force crossed the Beas, attacked, and utterly routed Ram Singh, who was occupying a strong position behind that river.

These services performed the Guides turned back, and hastening northwards arrived in the camp of the Grand Army in time to take part in the crowning and decisive victory of Gujrat. The battle, according to history, was chiefly an artillery duel, the preponderance and accuracy of our fire paving the way for a practically unchecked advance of the infantry. The Guides, therefore, did not see much fighting during the battle; but their turn came that night, when, attached to Gilbert's cavalry division, they joined in the strenuous pursuit of the Sikhs,--a pursuit which began on the battle-field and ended at the rocky gates of the Khyber two hundred miles away. The first burst carried the pursuing squadrons past the battle-field of Chillianwalla, across the Jhelum river, capturing on the way all the Sikh guns that had escaped from the battle-field. Snatching a few hours' rest, Gilbert's fine horsemen were again in the saddle, and with relentless fury hunted the demoralised enemy, allowing him not a moment's respite, not an hour to steady his flight or turn to bay. Right through the bright winter days, through a country of rocks and ravines, pressed on the avenging squadrons; till, utterly worn out, starving, with ammunition failing, a dejected and exhausted majority laid down their arms and surrendered unconditionally at Rawul Pindi. But the Affghan Horse in the service of the Sikhs fled still further north, hoping to escape to their own country, and in hot pursuit of these went the Guides, a stern stiff ride of close on a hundred miles; and running them staunchly to the end, they drove the sorry remnants across the Affghan border.

Thus brilliantly concluded the second Sikh War, which,

after many anxious moments and much hard fighting, resulted in adding to the Queen's domains a kingdom larger than France or Germany and more populous than Italy or Spain; and herein is recorded the modest share taken by the Guides in these great events.

## Chapter 3
# The Capture of the Fort of Gorindghar

A Traveller who at this day passes Amritsar by train will, if he looks to the south, see hard by the formidable fortress of Gorindghar. Over its battlements now floats the Union Jack, and on its drawbridge may be seen the familiar red coat of the British sentry. Should he ever pass that fort again, he may perhaps regard it with greater interest after reading the stirring tale of how it was captured from the Sikhs by a handful of resolute men of the Guides. To tell this story we must be forgiven for forsaking strict chronology; for the incident here narrated took place while part of the corps was still engaged at the siege of Mooltan.

Against modern artillery the fort of Gorindghar would be of little avail, however gallantly held; but by the standard of 1848 it was a very powerful work. Its armament consisted of no less than eighteen guns, while fifty-two lay stored in reserve, and its garrison consisted of such veteran fighters as a regiment of Sikh infantry. As may readily be understood, without touching on strategical details, it was a matter of considerable importance that this fort, lying as it did on the main line of the British communications between Umballa and Lahore, should not remain in hostile hands. It was therefore resolved to send back from Lahore a force to capture if possible, but at any rate to mask, this formidable work. To accomplish this, a considerable force was despatched from Lahore, and in advance of it was sent a party to reconnoitre and gain intelligence. This party consisted of Subadar[5] Rasul Khan, and one hundred and forty of all ranks of the Guides' infantry, with orders to get along as fast as they could. At noon, therefore, on a hot September day the little party set off on their forty mile march along the dusty, treeless road to Amritsar.

Marching all that day, and the greater part of the following night, Rasul Khan arrived in the vicinity of the fort just as day was breaking. His orders were to reconnoitre and find out in what state of preparedness the garrison stood, what was its strength in men and guns, the best means of attack, and the most vulnerable quarter. To gain all this useful information the most obviously complete method was to get inside the fort itself, and this the resourceful subadar determined to do.

It must be remembered that at this time the second Sikh war was in full swing, and that various bands of troops who had espoused the Sikh cause were roaming the country. The British forces, on the other hand, consisted chiefly of drilled and organised regiments, armed, equipped, and clothed on a regular basis, and recognisable as such. The Guides, however, newly raised, and living a rough and ready adventurous life in their ragged and war-worn khaki, bore little resemblance to these, and might to a casual observer come from anywhere, and belong to either side.

Rasul Khan was quick to perceive this point in his favour, and take full advantage of it; for during the long and weary night march, he had thought out his plan. Taking three of his own men, stripping off what uniform they had, and concealing their arms, he had them securely bound and placed under a heavy guard of their own comrades. As soon as it was broad daylight, closely guarding his prisoners, Rasul Khan marched boldly up to the main gate of the fort,

---

5. Subadar, a native commissioned officer commanding a company of infantry.

and was hailed by the Sikh sentry: "Halt there! who are you and what is your business?"

"After an exceedingly arduous pursuit, as you may judge from our dusty and exhausted condition," replied Rasul Khan, "we have managed to capture three most important prisoners, on whose heads a high price has been placed by the Sikh Durbar. They are the most desperate ruffians, full of the wiles of Satan, and we greatly fear lest they should escape us. I and my troops are weary, and to guard them in the open requires so many men. Of your kindness ask your Commandant if, in the Maharaja's name, I may place them in your guard-room cells until we march on again."

The Sikh sentry called the havildar[6] of the guard, who in turn called the Commandant, and after much palavering and cross questioning, the drawbridge was let down and the party admitted. The remainder of the Guides bivouacked here and there under the shade of the fort walls, cooked their food, and lay about at seeming rest, but all the while as alert and wide-awake as their extremely hazardous position required.

The guard-room cells were pointed out to Rasul Khan, the prisoners thrust into them, and the escort quietly but firmly invited to rejoin their comrades outside the walls; for in time of war, as the Commandant explained, it behoves every man, especially when the safety of a great fort is concerned, to walk warily, and treat the stranger with circumspection. So far, beyond seeing the main entrance and the guard-room cells, Rasul Khan had not done much towards securing that full information about the fort, its garrison, and its defences, which it was of such vital importance to gain. He had, however, secured a footing, and, while with apparent readiness he prepared to rejoin his men outside, he politely insisted that he must leave his own sentry to

---

6. Havildar, a native non-commissioned officer of infantry, corresponding to a sergeant.

guard the prisoners; "for," as he jocularly remarked to the Commandant, "if I don't, you will be saying that you captured these villains, and, sending them off to Lahore, will secure the reward my men have earned!" The Commandant laughed heartily at this blunt pleasantry, and partly out of good nature, and partly to avoid all blame should the prisoners escape, agreed to the proposal of the diplomatic subadar. During the course of the day the utmost cordiality was maintained, the Sikhs coming out and freely fraternising with the Guides, who, in their casual wanderings round, had at any rate got hold of a fairly shrewd notion of what the outside of the fort was like. But this was not enough for Rasul Khan, and he laid his further plans accordingly.

The cordial interchange of rough soldierly amenities had borne its fruit, and the suspicions of the Sikhs were completely lulled. To an alert and resourceful soldier like Rasul Khan, a man whom nothing in warlike strategy escaped, it occurred amongst other things that only a single sentry with his reliefs, under a non-commissioned officer, guarded the main entrance. As night fell, with engaging candour he pointed out the weakness of this arrangement to the Commandant, and, to avoid imposing additional guard duties on the Sikh garrison, offered, now that his men were well rested, to place a double sentry on the cells of the prisoners. Further, he made the obvious suggestion that it would be unsound, when once the drawbridge was up, to let it down each time that a relief of sentries was required, and that therefore it would probably be more convenient for all parties, as well as safer, if the reliefs for the double sentry also slept in the fort. With a whole regiment in garrison there seemed to be no particular objection to this proposal, and it was therefore accepted. Rasul Khan thus had at the main gate six men and a non-commissioned officer, not to mention three soldiers disguised as prisoners, as against three Sikhs and a non-commissioned officer. Be assured that he chose the bravest of the brave for that night's work, for, when the drawbridge was drawn slowly up that evening, it was ten men, and three of them unarmed, against a regiment; and short and terrible would have been the shrift accorded to them had an inkling of suspicion arisen, or had the slightest blunder, or precipitation, exposed the true position.

Meanwhile the force of cavalry and infantry sent by the British Resident was hastening down from Lahore, and Rasul Khan calculated that it would arrive at streak of dawn next morning. He despatched therefore two or three of his men to meet the column, to apprise the commanding officer of the state of affairs, urging him to make all haste and giving him as full information as possible should he on his arrival find that during the night disaster had fallen on the staunch little band of Guides. "On the other hand," the message concluded, "if by the Grace of God my plans prevail, I shall be ready to welcome your Honour at the fort gates at dawn."

To the party inside the fort the subadar's orders were to keep a very desultory watch over the prisoners, thus by example discouraging any undue vigilance on the part of the Sikh sentry; and for the rest to await quietly their opportunity till near dawn of day. This they did, and when the appointed hour had arrived the double sentry of the Guides fell like the upper millstone on that heedless Sikh sentry, and hewed him to the ground; at the same moment the rest of the guard was silently overpowered, gagged, and bound. Then, arming the three prisoners with the captured weapons, the Guides' sentries quickly and quietly lowered the drawbridge and let in the whole company of their comrades. Thus collected inside, with fixed bayonets, the cavalier, which commanded the whole of the interior of the work, was captured; the rest was easy, and the Sikhs, out-manoeuvred and placed at great disadvantage, surrendered at discretion. It is not always that the best laid plans succeed without a hitch, but the fortune of war was on this occasion entirely kind to the British cause, and the bold game played by subadar Rasul Khan and his men reaped a splendid reward; the capture of a formidable fortress, seventy guns, and a regiment of infantry, with little or no loss.

When, as dawn grew stronger, the British commander strained his anxious eyes towards the fort, to his immense relief friendly signals welcomed him, and as the sun rose the gentle breeze flung to the dusty haze the Union Jack, which ever since that day has floated from the ramparts of the fort of Gorindghar at Amritsar.

It may not be without interest, as illustrating the liberality with which soldiers in those days were treated, to mention that, besides the official thanks of the British Government, Rasul Khan received a robe of honour, a gun, a brace of pistols, and five hundred rupees, each havildar and naik fifty rupees, and each sepoy, including the "prisoners," eleven rupees. Nor may it be inappropriate to mention that Rasul Khan was a brother of that same ressaldar Fatteh Khan, who only the month before with a handful of the Guides' cavalry had scattered as chaff before the wind the flower of Diwan Mulraj's horsemen, and chased them into the gates of Mooltan.

# Chapter 4
# On the Frontier in the 'Fifties

The Guides were now two years old, and, as an outward and visible sign that they had won their spurs, they were by the orders of the Government considerably augmented. Hitherto with one troop and two companies they had established an honoured record; they were now raised to three troops of cavalry and six companies of infantry.

To the general historian, who can of necessity deal only with great events, peace reigned in India from the conclusion of the Sikh Wars to the outbreak of the Mutiny; but there was no peace for the Guides during those eight years. Their history is full of hardy adventure, of forced marches, and night attacks; of the wiles of the border free-lance, met and overcome with equal strategy and greater skill; of brave deeds and splendid devotion. The conscientious scribe is tempted to enlarge on each and all of these; but perhaps our purpose in giving the story of the Guides will be well enough served if we content ourselves with taking only two or three of these exploits, thus hoping to throw some light on the life led by a regiment on the Indian frontier in those rough days.

Dipping haphazard into the ancient records, we chance again on our old and gallant friend Fatteh Khan, Khuttuk; and once again we find him a man not easily taken aback in a sudden emergency. It was towards the end of 1851 that the British Government, having undertaken the surveying and mapping out of the Peshawur Valley and Yusafzai, deputed Mr. James, of the Survey Department, to superin-

A Picquet of the Guides' Infantry bivouacking

tend a portion of the work. For his protection during this duty, amongst a people fanatically opposed to anything in the shape of a map or a survey, a party of thirty of the Guides' cavalry was detailed under Ressaldar Fatteh Khan. This detachment was ordered to meet Mr. James at a small village named Gujar Garhi, about two miles from Mardan. Here, therefore, Fatteh Khan encamped to await the Sahib's arrival; but the day passed, the night fell, and still there were no signs of him. Thinking that there must have been some mistake in the dates, all turned in, and the camp was soon wrapped in slumber, the silence disturbed only by the stamping and roaring of the stallions at their standings, and by the crisp alert call of the sentries as they challenged.

It was past midnight, when a sharp-eyed Pathan sentry espied mistily through the darkness what looked like a large body of mounted men approaching. Instantly a sharp peremptory challenge rang out: "Halt! Who goes there?" Equally promptly floated back the answering watchword, "Friend." "What friend?" the sentry shouted, suspicious still. "Sahib," came back the disarming reply. Whereupon the sentry, coming to the not unnatural conclusion that the long-expected Sahib had at last arrived, and that he saw before him Mr. James with a large escort, sloped his sword, and gave the usual right of way: "Pass friend,--all's well."

At this moment Fatteh Khan awoke, and hearing the word sahib, jumped up, ran out of his tent, and hastened down to the end of the camp to meet the Sahib. He had, however, no sooner arrived there, than he at once noticed that the advancing horsemen were armed with matchlocks. Now our own cavalry in those days carried swords and lances, but not firearms, therefore these midnight visitors could not belong to any regiments in our service. To a man like Fatteh Khan, born to wars and alarms, who takes little for granted in daylight and nothing at night, this was sufficient to place him on his guard. With instant presence of mind he shouted, in a voice to be heard throughout the camp: "Rouse up everyone! Draw swords! The enemy are upon us!"

Scarcely had he ceased speaking when the enemy, throwing off further disguise, gave a yell and dashed at the camp, firing heavily as they rode. But though taken at a great disadvantage, and with odds of seven to one against them, the Guides made shift to be ready for the onslaught. There was naturally no time to get to horse, or into any regular formation, and therefore the attack had to be met on foot with sword and lance, in some hasty serviceable formation. Fatteh Khan therefore shouted to all the non-commissioned officers, who carried lances, to dash to the front and hold the outskirts of the camp, while the rank and file who were armed with swords should fall into knots of five or six, and prepare to defend themselves.

Against this hardy improvised defence the fierce attacks spent themselves like stormy waves against outstanding rocks; yet as a proof of the heavy fire, no tent escaped with less than ten or twelve bullet-holes. When once, however, the first fusillade was over, matters were on a somewhat more equal basis, for a matchlock cannot be reloaded on horseback; yet the odds were still great, and it took the Guides all their time to hold their own. But the surprise, as a surprise, having failed, the Swati cavalry, finding so stout a resistance, began to weaken in their endeavour. Catching the tide on the turn, the Guides dashed forth, and became themselves the attackers, hamstringing the horses, and so hewing, cutting, and thrusting, that, finding this no pigeons' nest, but rather a swarm of angry hornets, the whole two hundred horsemen scattered and fled.

The loss of the Guides in this staunch little affair proved, when all was over, to have been altogether insignificant; while the enemy on their part, besides leaving many dead men and horses in camp, carried off also, as was afterwards ascertained, a goodly number who would never throw a leg over a horse again. The leader of the attack was the redoubtable Mukaram Khan, one of the most daring and notable free-lances on the border.

In consequence of this and other raids it was determined to take measures, on a considerable scale, to discourage further efforts on the part of the border tribes. Consequently a brigade of all arms, under Sir Colin Campbell, moved out from Peshawur, to punish the lawless, and to exact retribution from those who had erred from the strict path of peace.

Amongst the various strongholds that were on the black list, and which, unless they surrendered at discretion, were destined to be attacked, captured, and sacked, was the Utmankheyl fortified village of Nawadand. Opposite this the British force sat down with the studied deliberation of old-time warfare, when contending armies might encamp for weeks and months within a stone's throw of each other. During this dignified pause, while doubtless supplies were being collected, and negotiations proceeding with the enemy, the British outpost line lay in full view of, and only "one shout's distance," as the Pathans expressively call it, from the enemy. And outside the line of infantry outposts lay a cavalry picket of twenty men of the Guides.

Thus it happened that one fine morning, in the month of May, 1852, the enemy, whether with intent to surprise, or merely fired with the nervous irritation of one who can no longer stand the strain of awaiting an impending blow, determined to hasten the issue by taking the offensive. So collecting his rough and ragged legions, stout of heart and stout of arm, carrying weapons not meanly to be compared with our own, the outlaw chief, Ajun Khan, marched out to attack the British, and to take them unawares in their tents.

The movement was at once reported by the British outposts, but troops take some few minutes to arm, equip, and form up in line of battle; while the Affghan border warrior moves with a swiftness that may well cause panic and dismay. A young subaltern of the Guides, Lieutenant G.N. Hardinge, seeing how matters were trending, rode out to the outlying picket of the Guides' cavalry, and there took his stand. It was an anxious moment. Behind him was the hastily arming camp, humming with the bustle of preparation; and before him, advancing across the stony plain, moved a line of skirmishers backed up by closed supports, and followed by great hordes of shouting warriors.

The motionless troop of the Guides stood foremost to meet the shock. On came the hardy tribesmen swiftly and relentlessly; but still, as he looked anxiously back, it was plain to the British subaltern that his comrades were not yet armed to meet the coming storm. "We can only give them one minute more," he said, and stout and steady came the answer: "Yes, your Honour, one minute more." And as they spoke each stalwart trooper gripped his sword still tighter and, shortening his reins, laid the flat of his thigh hard on his wiry neighing stallion; for as of old, so now, the war-horse scented the battle from afar.

The time passed very slowly, a minute seeming an eternity to the impatient soldiers. Fifteen seconds--twenty seconds--thirty seconds--forty-five seconds--sixty!

"Carry swords," in a serene and conversational voice remarked the young subaltern; equally smoothly and quietly came the order, "Walk, march." Then, as the troop moved forward, followed the slightly more animated command, "Trot"; and as the excitement of coming conflict coursed with the wild exuberance of youth through the boy's veins, "Gallop! Charge!" he yelled, and back came an answering shout, "Fear not, Sahib, we are with you!" And thus was launched on the flood of death a little band of heroes, that they might save an army.

But ever since the day when David slew Goliath, the God of Battles has not always sided with the big battalions. A few staunch hearts hurled fearlessly at the foe may still, like the ancient slinger's stone, lay low the giant. So on this occasion the effect of the bold attack was magical. Through the thin line of skirmishers, heedless of the spluttering fire, went the troop, like a round shot through a paper screen, and fell like yelling furies on the clumps of swordsmen, pikemen, and any-weapon-men, who formed the supports. These they killed and wounded and scattered like chaff to the wind. And then,--their mission was accomplished! The enemy's advancing masses wavered, halted, hesitation and dismay replacing the confident sling-trot of a few minutes before. The surprise had failed, the camp was saved. Then Hardinge, his work accomplished, himself sore wounded, the enemy's standard in his hands, rallied his pursuing troop, and clearing to a flank left displayed the British force drawn up and ready to receive all comers.

To see the right moment and to seize it, to balance the profit and loss, counting one's own life as a feather in the scales, to strike hard and bold whatever the odds,--such are a few simple soldier lessons, learnt not from the scribes, but from a gallant British subaltern.

\* \* \* \* \*

While Lieutenant Lumsden was in England in 1853 the command of the Guides was given to Lieutenant W.S.R. Hodson. This book would not be complete without relating the story of at any rate one of the many occasions on which this gallant officer, afterwards so famous, showed his fine metal. The fight about to be described was one, too, in which the many brave and devoted officers who have been surgeons to the corps have displayed the greatest gallantry.

For high crimes and misdemeanours it was decided to punish the large and important cluster of villages named Bori, in the land of the Jowaki Afridis, not far from the present military station of Cherat. A brigade of all arms, consisting of the 22nd Foot, 20th Punjab Infantry, 66th Gurkhas (now the 1st Gurkha Rifles), the Corps of Guides, a squadron of Irregular Cavalry, some 9-pounder guns on elephants, and a company of Sappers, the whole under Colonel S.B. Boileau, was detailed for the undertaking. The Bori villages lay in the valley of the same name enclosed by high and rugged mountains, making both ingress and egress in face of practised mountaineers a most difficult operation.

The advance was led by the Guides, who, themselves active as panthers in the hills, drove the Afridis before them through the Bori villages and up the precipitous mountains behind. The main body then set to work to burn and destroy the villages with all the food and fodder therein, and to drive off the cattle. So far, as is often the case in fighting these mountaineers, all had gone well; but now came the crucial time. Afridis may be driven all day like mountain sheep, but when the night begins to fall, and their tired pursuers commence of necessity to draw back to lower levels for food and rest, then this redoubtable foe rises in all his strength, and with sword and gun and huge boulder hurls himself like a demon on his retiring enemy.

At one of the furthest points ahead was Lieutenant F. McC. Turner, who with about thirty men of the Guides had driven a very much superior force of the enemy into a stone breastwork at the top of a high peak. Here the British officer was held; not an inch could he advance; and now he was called upon to conform with the general movement for retirement. To retire, placed as he was, meant practical annihilation, so sticking to the rocks like a limpet he blew a bugle calling for reinforcement. Hodson, who himself was faced by great odds, seeing the serious position of his friend, sent across all the men he could afford to extricate him, but these were not strong enough to effect their purpose. Then it was that Dr. R. Lyell, the surgeon of the Guides, took on himself to carry forward the much needed succour. In reserve lying near him was the Gurkha company of the Guides, and also a company of the 66th Gurkhas under a native officer. Taking these troops, with great dash and personal gallantry he led them to the attack, drove back the already exulting enemy, stormed their position, and extricated Lieutenant Turner and his party from their perilous position. It was a noble deed, nobly and gallantly carried out; and when it had been achieved, the brave fighter returned to the tender care of the wounded, and to alleviate the pains of the dying.

And now Hodson had got together the threads of his retirement, and using one to help the other, gradually and slowly drew back, covering the brigade with a net of safety. Thus quietly falling back, and meeting wild charges with ball and bayonet, he kept the open valley till all the force had safely passed the defile of exit. Then, while the last of his infantry got safely to commanding posts on the lower slopes, he himself, with the ready resource of the born fighter, changed his game, and from the patient rôle of the steady infantry commander, became a cavalry leader. Mounting his horse and calling on the Guides' cavalry to follow him, he suddenly charged the astonished enemy, and hurling them back with slaughter secured for the rest of his men a peaceful retirement. But before they laid themselves on the hard ground, this paladin of the fight and his staunch warriors had spent eighteen hours in desperate warfare with little food and no water.

So far as the records show this was the first occasion on which Hodson had led a cavalry charge, and was an auspicious opening to a cavalry career of remarkable brilliancy,-

-a career which was brought to a brave, but untimely end, only four years later before the walls of Lucknow.

Amongst other historic figures who watched this fight, and who added their generous meed of praise, were John Lawrence, the saviour of the Punjab, who later, as Lord Lawrence, was Viceroy of India, Major Herbert Edwardes, now Commissioner of Peshawur, who as a subaltern had won two pitched battles before Mooltan, and Lieutenant-Colonel Robert Napier, afterwards Lord Napier of Magdala and Commander-in-Chief of the Army in India.

# Chapter 5
# The Story of Dilawur Khan

The story of Dilawur Khan, subadar of the Guides, is one which kindles many a kindly memory of the rough brave fellows who, under a sprinkling of English officers, upheld British supremacy on the North-West Frontier of India in the early 'fifties.

When Lumsden was raising the Guides he looked about for men who, as he expressed it, were "accustomed to look after themselves and not easily taken aback by any sudden emergency,"--men born and bred to the sword, who had faced death a hundred times from childhood upwards, and who had thus instinctively learnt to be alert, brave, and self-reliant. To these hardy warriors Lumsden explained the simple doctrine that they were enlisted for three years, had to do what they were bid, and would receive a certain fixed salary every month for their trouble.

Soldiers of fortune and dashing young bloods from all the countryside flocked to his standard, and so popular was the corps that there were sometimes as many as thirty of these receiving no pay, and maintaining themselves and their horses, while awaiting a vacancy. And great indeed was the excitement when Lumsden, in his bluff breezy way, would say: "Well, here's a vacancy, and I don't for the life of me know which of you to give it to. Come along down to the rifle-range, and shoot it off amongst yourselves; the best shot gets the vacancy." And off they would go to the range, with all their friends and relations to the fifth generation, and all the partisans in the corps of each competitor: shooting for the King's Prize at Bisley is a flat and tame proceeding in comparison with this. And as each shot was fired the friends of the competitor would yell: "Shahbash! Bravo! Well shot! Another bull's eye! You will win for certain." While rival interests would with equal emphasis discredit the performance: "This bull's eye was certainly an accident. God willing he will miss next time. Bravo! let us not lose heart!"

The demeanour of the winner on such occasions would make a Master in Lunacy look grave. The happy young fellow would jump into the air, yelling and pirouetting, brandishing a sword, and at frequent intervals letting off a gun, nominally into the air, while most of his friends did likewise, embracing and congratulating him in the intervals. Without taking a seat amongst the Scribes and Pharisees, it is perhaps permissible to notice that such a scene as this is in curious contrast to that to be seen in any French or German country town when lots are being drawn for conscription. There the youth, who by drawing a lucky number escapes serving his country, is congratulated, fêted, and led in procession round the streets.

One hard and fast rule, however, Lumsden made. He would take no low caste men; he would have naught to say to the washermen, sweepers, and fiddlers[7] of the village; he would take only the highest, which in this land is the fighting caste. His argument was one which still holds good. It is not in reason to expect the classes which for hundreds of years have been hewers of wood and drawers of water, and for hundreds of years have been accustomed to receive the cuffs and kicks of their village superiors, to face readily the fighting classes in the day of battle. The prestige of the soldier would be wanting to them, and prestige counts for as much in the East as elsewhere.

Yet holding these views, a brave man was a brave man

---

7. A musician in India is a low caste person.

to Lumsden, be his birth or caste what it might be. Most English-speaking people have read Mr. Rudyard Kipling's poem about Gunga Din the bhisti, or water-carrier, who by the unanimous verdict of the soldiers was voted the bravest man in the battle. Whether Mr. Kipling got that incident from the Guides or not his poem does not show, but there it actually occurred. The name of the bhisti was Juma, and so gallantly did he behave in action at Delhi, calmly carrying water to the wounded and dying under the most tremendous fire, that the soldiers themselves said: "This man is the bravest of the brave, for without arms or protection of any sort he is in the foremost line; if any one deserves the star for valour this man does." And so the highest distinction open to an Indian soldier was bestowed on Juma the bhisti; and further, the soldiers petitioned that he should be enlisted and serve in the ranks as a soldier, and no longer be menially employed. Nor was this all: in spite of his low birth, in a country where birth is everything, he rose step by step to be a native officer; and then to crown his glory, in the Afghan War he again won the star for valour, and the clasp which that great distinction carries. But this story is not about Juma, and so we must reluctantly leave him and get to our theme.

At this time it so happened that the most notorious highwayman and outlaw in the whole of Yusafzai was one Dilawur Khan, a Khuttuk of good family belonging to the village of Jehangira, on the Kabul River near its junction with the Indus. Brought up to the priesthood, his wild and impetuous nature and love of adventure could not brook a life of sedentary ease, and therefore, like many a spirited young blood, both before and since, he "took to the road." In his case the step was taken, if not actually with the sanction and blessing of his Church, at any rate with its unofficial consent. In those days the Sikhs held by force the country of the Faithful, and Hindus fattened on its trade. It was no great sin therefore, indeed, an active merit, that the sons of the Prophet, sword in hand, should spoil the Egyptian, by night or by day, as provided for by Allah.

To recount all the adventures of Dilawur would fill a book, and require a Munchausen to write it; but there was about them all a touch of humour, and sometimes of almost boyish fun, accompanied often by the rough courtesies of the gentlemen of the road, which reminds one of Dick Turpin and other famous exponents of the profession on the highways of England.

Now it so happened that it was at this time one of Lumsden's duties to hunt down and capture Dilawur, who for just and sufficient cause was now an outlaw, with a price on his head of no less than two thousand rupees. Many a time and oft did Lumsden and his men plan and strive, and ride and hide, but no nearer could they get to the capture of Dilawur.

Sitting one evening outside his tent, after yet another unsuccessful attempt, it suddenly occurred to Lumsden that Dilawur must have an astonishingly intimate knowledge of every path, nullah, and pass in the district to thus evade capture, as well as a remarkably efficient intelligence department, to give him timely warning. "Just the man for the Guides," exclaimed Lumsden. "I'll send for him." A polite note was accordingly written inviting Dilawur Khan to come into the Guides' camp, at any time and place that fitted in with his other, and doubtless more important, engagements, "to talk matters over." At the same time a free passport was sent which would allow of his reaching the camp unmolested. It speaks volumes for the high estimate which British integrity had already earned amongst these rough borderland people, that a man with two thousand rupees on his head could accept such an invitation. For the same man to have accepted a similar invitation from the Sikhs, or even from his own countrymen, would have been an act of culpable and aimless suicide.

One fine day, therefore, Dilawur strolled into camp, and he and Lumsden began "to talk matters over." After compliments, as the Eastern saying is, Lumsden with much heartiness, and in that free and easy manner which was his own, took Dilawur with the utmost candour into his confidence.

"Look here, Dilawur," said he; "you are a fine fellow, and are living a fine free life of adventure, and I daresay are making a fairly good thing out of it. So far, although I have done my best, I have failed to catch you, but catch you I assuredly shall some day. And what do you suppose I shall do with you when I do catch you? Why, hang you as high as Haman,--a gentleman whose history appears in our Good Book. Now, that's a poor ending for a fine soldier like you, and I'll make you an offer, take it or leave it. I'll enlist you, and as many of your men as come up to my standard, in the Guides, and with decent luck you will soon be a native officer, with good fixed pay, and a pension for your old age, and, meanwhile, as much fighting as the greatest glutton can wish for. Well, what do you say?"

Dilawur Khan first stared, thunderstruck at the novelty and unexpectedness of the offer; and then, tickled with the comical side of it, burst into a roar of laughter. It was one of the very best jokes he had ever heard. He, an outlaw, with a price on his head, his sins forgiven, enlisted in the Guides, with the prospect of becoming a native officer! "No, no," he exclaimed, "that won't do"; and, still shaking with laughter, rose to take his leave. And as he walked away he was followed by the hearty and genial voice of Lumsden roaring after him: "Mind, I'll catch you some day, Dilawur, and then I'll hang you, as sure as my name's Lumsden!"

Lumsden, having many other matters on hand, thought

nothing more about the matter, till, much to his surprise, one day six weeks later, who should walk calmly into his camp, without passport or safe conduct, or anything save serene confidence in the British officer, but Dilawur Khan.

"I've been thinking of what you said," he began, "and I have come to enlist, and as many of my band as you care to take."

"That's right," said Lumsden, with great affability. "I thought you were a sensible fellow, as well as a brave one. I'll take you on."

"I have, however, one condition to make," solemnly continued the outlaw.

"Well, what's that?" asked Lumsden, thinking that he was going to drive some desperate bargain.

"I'll enlist on one condition," replied Dilawur, "and that is, I must be let off doing the goose-step. I really can't stand about on one leg, a laughing-stock amongst a lot of recruits."

"Oh, nonsense," laughed Lumsden; "you'll have to begin at the beginning, like everyone else. The goose-step is one of the foundations of the British Empire. If a king came into the army he'd have to do it. Why, I had to do goose-step myself! Of course you'll have to do it."

So with much good-humoured laughing and chaffing Dilawur Khan enlisted; and for weeks after one of the sights of Yusafzai, which notable chiefs rode many a mile to see, was the dreaded Dilawur, the terror of the Border, peacefully balancing himself on one leg, under the careful tuition of a drill-sergeant of the Guides.

Long years afterwards, when he had reached the highest rank open to him, in one of his friendly talks with Lumsden, he said: "Yes, Sahib, when I enlisted I thought you were one of the most unsophisticated persons I had ever come across. All I took on for was to learn your tricks and strategy, and how British troops were trained, and how they made their bandobust[8] for war. Directly I had learnt these things I had intended walking off whence I came, to use my knowledge against my enemies. But by the kindness of God I soon learnt what clean and straight people the sahibs are, dealing fairly by all, and devoid of intrigue and underhand dealing. So I stopped on, and here I am, my beard growing white in the service of the Queen of England."

His early religious education had given Dilawur more than the average insight into the intricacies of Mahomedan doctrine, and being possessed of ready wit, and considerable ability in debate, he was ever anxious to enter into doctrinarian discussions with the mullahs. Their superstitions especially came in for his lively ridicule, and a good story is told by old native officers illustrating his views. One day, Dilawur with a crowd of other passengers was crossing the Indus, which there was very deep and rapid, in the ferryboat. Being over-heavily loaded, the boat, when it felt the strong current, appeared in great danger of filling and sinking. Then the Mahomedans on board with one accord set up loud lamentations, and began to call upon their saints to succour them. "Oh Ali! Oh Hosein! Oh Káka Sahib! save us," they cried. Whereupon Dilawur, not to be outdone, in his turn commenced yelling and shouting vociferously: "Lumsden Sahib! Oh Lumsden Sahib, save me!" "What are you doing, you accursed infidel?" exclaimed the scandalised passengers, furiously. "Why do you supplicate Lumsden Sahib? It is enough to sink the boat straight away." "That is easily explained," calmly replied Dilawur. "You are calling on saints who have been dead for ages, while Lumsden Sahib is alive and lives close by. Personally I consider it more sensible to call on a living man than on a dead saint."

---

8. Bandobust, lit., a tying or binding; any system or mode of regulation discipline; arrangements.

On another occasion his enthusiasm in the cause of religious enlightenment nearly cost him his life. When the Amir Dost Mahomed Khan came to Peshawur in 1856, he was accompanied by Hafiz Ji, a leading mullah of Afghanistan and a great doctrinarian; to whom came the learned amongst the Faithful, to discuss the tenets of their religion and to listen to the wisdom of the wise. With them came also Dilawur, full of zeal and thirsting for knowledge, who artlessly introduced so debatable a subject, that the assembly was thrown into an uproar; and lest worse things might happen unto him, the worthy, but too enquiring, subadar was hustled hastily forth, and requested in future to stick to soldiering, and to avoid bringing his infernal questions to cause discord amongst the chosen of the Prophet. As Dilawur afterwards pathetically remarked, he "didn't think much of a religion which instead of meeting argument with argument only threw stones at the head of the seeker after knowledge." Indeed the occasion seems to have thoroughly unsettled him in the convictions of his youth, for shortly afterwards he finally shook off all connection with the Mahomedan religion, and turning Christian was baptised at Peshawur in 1858.

During the Mutiny he did excellent service, making the famous march to Delhi with the Guides, and serving with them throughout the siege and storming of that place. He served also in the many skirmishes which occurred on the frontier during the next twelve years, getting what he had bargained for on joining, plenty of fighting. And then came that call of duty which asked of the staunch old warrior to lay down his life for the foreign Queen whose good servant he was.

In 1869 the British Government wanted a man to go on a special and important mission, a man of infinite resource, well educated, hardy and brave, for he would need to carry his life in his hands for many a long day and many a weary mile. The man selected was Dilawur Khan, and joyfully he undertook the risks and excitement of the service. With him went a comrade, Ahmed Jan, also of the Guides. The two set forth together, and after many hardships and adventures had reached the territory of the Mehtar of Chitral, and were nearing the completion of their task. Seated one day under a tree, making their midday halt and chatting with some fellow travellers, they were suddenly surrounded by the soldiers of the Mehtar and hurried back under close guard to Chitral. Seeing danger ahead, Dilawur, before he was searched, managed to drop into the river certain documents and reports of a secret nature, which it was important should not fall into strange hands.

On arrival at Chitral he and his companions were thrown into prison, there to await the Mehtar's pleasure. When eventually they were brought before him, that chieftain, addressing Dilawur, asked, "Who are you and whence come you?" "I am the Mullah Dilawur," replied the prisoner, "on my way from Bokhara on a religious mission."

"No, you are not," replied the Mehtar; "you are Subadar Dilawur of the Guides, a heretic and an infidel."

"Quite true," answered Dilawur readily; "I was at one time a subadar of the Guides, but I have been many things in my time, and now I am a mullah."

"I have reliable information," said the Mehtar, "that you are in the secret employment of the British Government."

"Go to," laughed Dilawur, "what next? I have a proposal to make. If you doubt that I am a mullah, and not an ignorant one, be pleased to call together all your most learned priests and I will discuss doctrine with them, till all are convinced."

"If you will confess and tell me the secrets of the Government," replied the Mehtar, "I will give you a handsome present and take you into my service."

"I have no secrets," said Dilawur, "and I beg of your Highness to allow me to proceed on my way. On my arrival at the ziarat[9] of the Káka Sahib near Nowshera I will make a special offering on behalf of your Highness, and extol your generosity."

But the Mehtar evidently had very straight information regarding Dilawur, and it was the custom of the land to kill all strangers who could not account for themselves, and more especially those who had any connection with the dreaded Feringhis. For the Pathan saying is: "First comes one Englishman, as a traveller or for shikar;[10] then come two and make a map; then comes an army and takes the country. It is better therefore to kill the first Englishman." Dilawur was consequently sent back to prison, and a meeting of the mullahs decided that he should be stoned to death as an apostate. "It must be the will of God," said this brave man when the news was brought him, and prepared to meet his fate.

But not yet was his time fulfilled. For two months he and his travelling companions were kept in prison, probably to enable the Mehtar to correspond with his agents in Peshawur. The reply received was evidently not in favour of extreme measures for the strong arm of the British was notoriously far-reaching, and serious trouble might ensue if the subadar were killed. The Mehtar therefore decided to release the prisoners, and to give them such assistance as they needed in getting away.

On their way towards India the little party got as far as the great range of mountains, some twenty-four thousand feet in height, which divide Chitral from Bajaur, and attempted to cross it by the Nuksan Pass, the Pass of Death. For four days and nights they struggled on, through the ever deepening snow and ever increasing cold. Dilawur

---

9. Ziarat, cemetery.
10. Shikar, sport.

Khan's comrade, Ahmed Jan, was the first to die; and then, on the fourth night, the brave old soldier himself gave out, and as he was dying he called to him one of the survivors, and said: "Should any of you reach India alive, go to the Commissioner of Peshawur and say 'Dilawur Khan of the Guides is dead'; and say also that he died faithful to his salt, and happy to give up his life in the service of the Great Queen."

So he died, and the eternal snows cover as with a soft and kindly sheet the rugged soldier who knew no fear. The serene and majestic silence of the mountain is given to him whose life in the plain below had been one great and joyous fight from the cradle to the grave.

Chapter 6
# The Great March to Delhi

For the Guides the great tragedy of 1857 opened with the mutiny of the 55th Native Infantry. When this regiment first showed signs of insubordination it was quartered at the neighbouring cantonment of Nowshera, then slenderly garrisoned by British troops, but with many European women and children. For safety's sake it was therefore thought better to isolate the regiment by sending it over to Mardan. With the news of the outbreak at Meerut the demeanour of the regiment became more sullen and menacing, and it was accordingly decided at once to disarm the sepoys. For this purpose a column was sent from Peshawur, consisting of a wing of the 70th Foot, a portion of the 5th Punjab Infantry under Vaughan, two hundred and fifty sabres of the 10th Irregular Cavalry, and some Mounted Police; the whole under Colonel Chute of the 70th Foot, with John Nicholson as political officer.

The 55th Native Infantry had been warned that the column was coming, and when, from the walls of the fort, they saw it approaching, they broke and fled, taking the Katlung road, thus hoping to escape across the border into Swat and Buner. Nicholson with the cavalry and mounted police immediately started in pursuit. The cavalry, themselves disaffected, did no execution whatever; but the police behaved with great dash and gallantry, killing one hundred and twenty, and capturing one hundred and fifty of the mutineers. The remainder escaped across the border, but their fate was only postponed. Some were murdered by the tribesmen, some driven back into British territory, captured and hanged, and some were blown from guns before the eyes of the garrison of Peshawur. Of the whole regiment all were destroyed except a few scores who escaped the gallows and the guns to suffer transportation for life. Such was the terrible ending of the 55th Native Infantry; a signal and, as it proved, a most effective warning, the results of which were felt over the whole of the north-west corner of India.

A distressing and pathetic tragedy resulted from the mutiny of this regiment. Colonel Henry Spottiswoode who commanded it, like so many other officers, absolutely refused to believe in the disloyalty of his men. He was one of those who held the view that distrust bred disaffection, which with confidence would never appear. So deeply distressed was this chivalrous officer when his regiment rebelled, that he refused to outlive what to him was an indelible disgrace, and so, going apart, shot himself dead. According to an old soldier, then in the Guides, he fell and was buried under a great mulberry tree at the cross-roads near the fort.

Meanwhile, the Guides, at six hours' notice, fully equipped, horse and foot, had started on their historic march to Delhi. They left Mardan at six in the evening of May 13th, and joined the British force at the siege of Delhi early on June 9th. The distance is five hundred and eighty miles, and the time taken was twenty-six days and fourteen hours; but from this must be deducted five days and nine hours made up as follows: detained forty-two hours at Attock, holding the fort pending the arrival of a reliable garrison; detained forty-one hours at Rawul Pindi, pending the question as to whether the Guides were to be employed to disarm the native artillery; detained forty-six hours at Karnal by the magistrate, in order to attack, capture, and burn a hostile village lying twelve miles off the road. If, therefore, these halts "by order" are deducted, it will be found that the Guides took actually twenty-one days and five hours to march five hundred and eighty miles. This works out to an average of over twenty-seven miles a day. As a contemporary historian remarks, such a feat would be highly creditable to mounted troops, and was doubly so to the infantry portion of the corps. To add to the credit of this high achievement, it may be added that the march took place at the hottest season of the year through the hottest region on earth.

The record of a march along the Grand Trunk Road of India does not lend itself to much picturesque description, but perhaps it may be in this case of some interest to follow the stern resolve and steady endurance which carried the stout-hearted regiment through those never-ending miles along the straight and scorching road to Delhi. And in this endeavour we are singularly fortunate in having for reference a diary written from day to day by Henry Daly, who, in the absence of Lumsden on a special mission, commanded the corps.[11]

The first night's march took the Guides sixteen miles to Nowshera, where after barely two hours' rest came orders to push on to Attock, another eighteen miles. To add to the hardships of this march, it so chanced that the Mahomedan fast of Ramzan was in observance, during which no follower of the Prophet may eat or drink between sunrise and sunset. Parched, hungry, and weary, the thirty-four mile march was completed, and the Indus crossed at ten in the morning of the 14th of May.

Halting by order forty-two hours at Attock, to allow of the arrival of a relief garrison, the Guides pushed on thirty-two miles to Burhan, on the night of the 15th--16th, in the midst of a violent dust storm. Many of the men were very footsore from their long march of the pre-

---

11. Memoirs of General Sir Henry Dermot Daly, G.C.B., C.I.E.; by Major H. Daly. London, 1905.

vious day, but all were cheerful and light-hearted, making naught of their hardships.

Another thirty-two mile march brought the corps to Jani-ki-Sang, and took them the next morning fifteen miles in to Rawul Pindi. On the road Herbert Edwardes passed the corps, and drove Daly on into Rawul Pindi, there to meet the great hearts of the Punjab, John Lawrence, Neville Chamberlain, and John Nicholson.

A day was spent here in consultation on the broad aspect of affairs, and locally as to the advisability, or otherwise, of using the Guides to disarm the native artillery in garrison. Finally it was decided not to do so, and thus with the gruff but kindly farewells of John Lawrence, and the light-hearted chaff and high spirits of Herbert Edwardes, Daly and his men again set forth, and on the night of the 19th--20th made a twenty mile march to Mandra. There was no falling off in the cheerful endeavour, nor was any man so tired or footsore that he would be content to be left behind.

The next march brought the corps to Sohawa, twenty-four miles, made trying by hot scorching winds and the deep and intricate nullahs which had to be crossed. Then followed twenty-eight miles, and in delightful contrast the vicinity of great rushing waters made a little heaven of the camp on the banks of the Jhelum. But it was not for long; at dusk trumpets and bugles again sound the advance, and amidst a great storm of dust and rain the second of the great rivers of the Punjab is crossed, and in addition to the great difficulty and delay of a night passage, yet another twenty-one miles are added to the marching score before daylight. The 24th being a cooler day, Daly resolved to push on another fifteen miles to the Chenab, and to cross that river during the course of the night. This was safely accomplished, and by early morning on the 24th all were on the eastern bank at Wazirabad. That night the men were called upon for another thirty-two mile march, and daylight saw them at Kamoké. Resting all day nightfall again found them on the road completing another thirty miles into Lahore, the capital of the Punjab. The hour was six in the morning, and the date the 26th of May, from which it will be seen that the Guides had so far covered two hundred and sixty-seven miles in ten and a half marching-days.

At Lahore Daly picked up some recruits to replace casualties, as well as to have a few in hand to meet future vacancies. Marching on, the banks of the Sutlej, close to the battlefield of Sobraon, forty-three miles from Lahore, were reached early on the 29th, and the passage of this, the fifth great river of the Punjab, was at once commenced. Then on again at dusk thirty-two more miles to Mihna; a more than usually trying march this, for a cross-country road caused many to lose their way, and it was twenty-four hours before all the baggage was in. This necessitated making the next a short march, in order that all might get into trim again; so at midnight, at the fourteenth milestone, Daly called a halt, and all slept the sleep of those who have endured much. June 1st saw the corps march into Ludhiana at three in the morning, after covering twenty-four miles. Here all was silence, and the officers, using the lowest step of the courthouse as a pillow, slept soundly till dawn.

A pleasant restful day in the great cool house of the Deputy Commissioner, Mr. Ricketts, with such unheard of luxuries as cold water and iced ginger-beer to drink, and cool sheets to lie on, put fresh vigour into the little band of British officers, and off they went at half-past seven in the evening for a twenty-eight mile march to Alawi-ke-Serai. Another march, next night, of the same distance brought the corps to Rajpoora. They were now close to Umballa, and another night march brought them, at one in the morning of June 4th, to the deserted cantonment.

Here they were received in friendly fashion by the troopers of the Maharaja of Patiala, who had been left in charge,

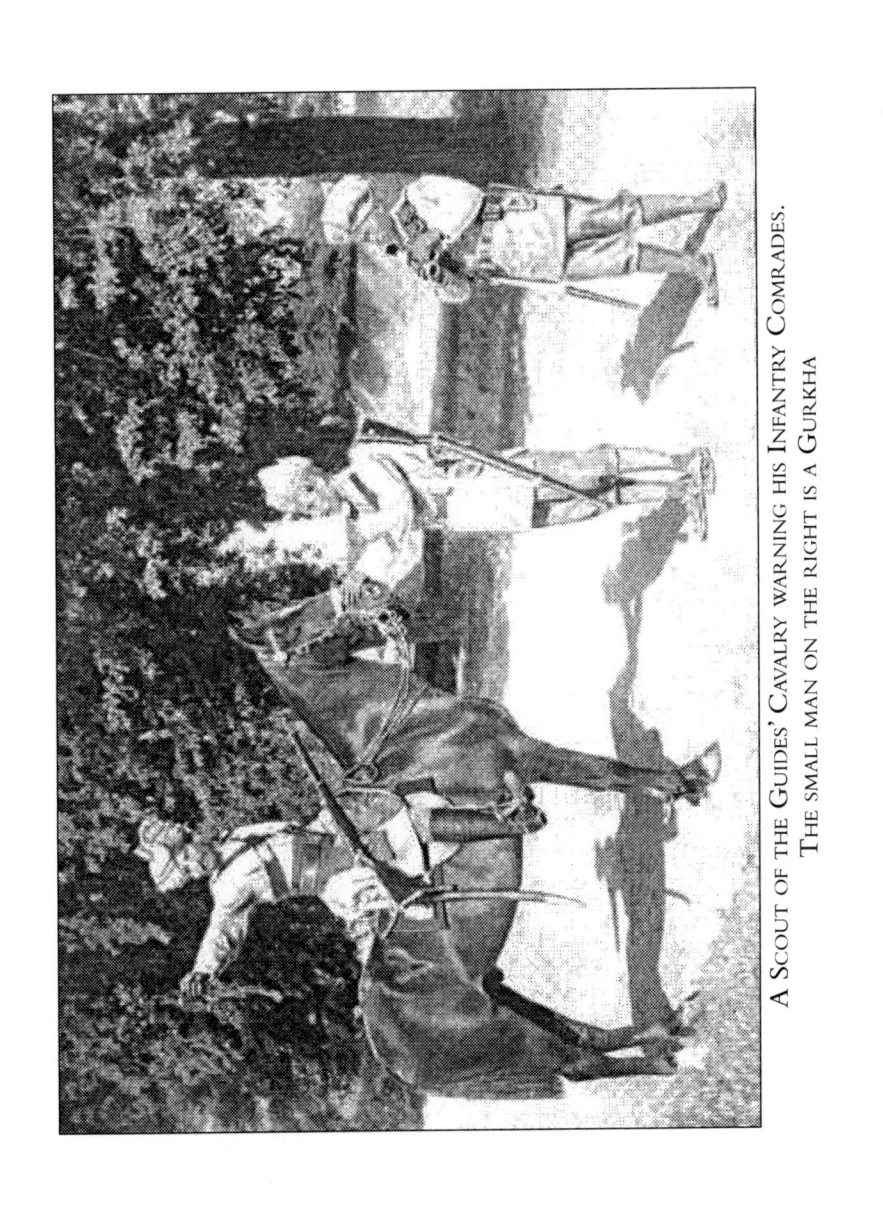

A Scout of the Guides' Cavalry warning his Infantry Comrades. The small man on the right is a Gurkha

and were conducted to a grove of great trees near a tank, probably in the vicinity of the present racecourse. After a good day's rest under the trees the march was continued to Pipli, twenty-six miles, where a letter was received from Mr. Barnes, the Commissioner, giving news of the force at Meerut, and inferring that they were not much more than holding their own.

At Karnal, twenty-four miles onward, and now nearing their goal, two causes of delay crossed their path. Cholera, that ancient scourge of the East which finds its easiest prey when men are physically impoverished with great exertions, now attacked the dusty road-worn corps, three Gurkhas being the first victims, while seven or eight more men were down the same evening. At the same time came a call from Mr. Le Bas, the magistrate, strongly backed by Sir Theophilus Metcalfe, to turn aside in order to burn a mutinous village. Greatly demurring at any delay in reaching his main objective, the demand was so urgent that Daly felt bound to comply with it. His compliance cost him small loss, but the delay cost the British cause the help of the Guides at the battle of Budlika-Serai. Though too late for that fight, however, they were in time for many another before the walls of Delhi.

The moral effect of the arrival of the Guides in Delhi was perhaps in some measure greater even than the actual fighting strength thus brought into line. The fame of the march from the far distant frontier, the fine physique and martial bearing of soldiers drawn from warlike tribes new to the eyes of their British comrades, the encouraging and enheartening effect of the arrival of reinforcements however small, all tended to give the approach of the travel-stained Guides a high significance. Some such thought perhaps intuitively occurred to all; and every soldier who could claim to be off duty rushed to the dusty road-side, and hoarsely cheered the gallant fellows who had overcome so much to reach the side of their British comrades, hard set to uphold the great Empire of Clive and Warren Hastings. It is interesting, at this distance of time, to find recorded the impression of an eye-witness who was amongst those who watched and cheered as the Guides, after a last thirty mile march, strode manfully into the camp at Delhi, on this, the morning of the 9th of June, 1857. "Their stately height and martial bearing," says this onlooker, "made all who saw them proud to have such aid. They came in as firm and light as if they had marched but a single mile."

At the end of this great march rest and peace for a day or two had assuredly been earned. But no; as the Guides approach the historic Ridge, a staff officer, sent out to meet them, gallops up, and after giving friendly greeting, with the General's compliments, asks, "How soon will you be ready to go into action?" "In half an hour," is the gallant Daly's cheery reply. And thus it came about that history added one more touch of glory to a great achievement. A little space of time there was for partial rest and hard-earned food, and then the trumpet calls to seize their arms and face the foe they had come so far to fight. And in that fight both horse and foot showed great and glorious valour; but when evening came, and beaten back the rebels hid behind the walls of Delhi, the roll-call told its sad undying story. Full many a Guide had made that strenuous march but to lay down his life e'er yet he had pitched his tent. And brightest lights, as was meet, amidst these heroes, were the little band of British officers, for of those, in that one first fight, all were killed or wounded. Amongst the latter was the lion-hearted, ever-cheerful Daly; and amongst the former the first of the great soldier-name of Battye to die a soldier's death. And as he died in that great agony his face lit up, and calm and smooth came the grand old Roman verse:

*Dulce et decorum est pro patria mori.*

The story of the Guides before Delhi is the story of

all that gallant band who through the blazing heat, 'midst sickness and disease, fought the good fight right through the summer of 1857, and with them shared in the crowning glory of the final assault and capture of the capital of the Great Mogul. Hence after a few months' harrying and chasing of rebel bands, with sadly diminished numbers, but still stout of heart, the order came for the Guides to return to their home on the distant frontier.

In the midst of so much treachery, such dastardly deeds of murder and rapine, the bright light of unwavering fidelity, sealed and confirmed by surpassing gallantry in the field, so appealed to the hearts of the storm-pressed Englishmen, that the Guides received little short of an ovation when they returned to Peshawur. By order of Major-General Sir Sidney Cotton the whole of the garrison was paraded to receive the shattered remnants of that war-worn corps. On their approach a royal salute was fired by the artillery, and cavalry and infantry came to the salute while the massed bands played. The General then made a most eloquent and affecting address, welcoming the corps back to the frontier, and expressing the pride and honour felt by all in being associated with men whose deeds of daring had earned for themselves and their noble profession undying fame. They had taken six hundred men to Delhi and their casualties had reached three hundred and fifty. During the siege the whole strength in British officers had been renewed four times, and all these had been killed or wounded. One officer indeed had been wounded six times and yet survived, another four times, and others at least twice.

After his stirring speech, the General called for three cheers for the little band of ragged and war-worn heroes, who stood before them. A *feu de joie* accompanied by a salute of twenty-one guns was then fired, and after this the Guides, taking the place of honour at the head of the line, marched past the flag.

# Chapter 7
# Twenty Years of Minor Wars

Short breathing space, and little of the rest of peace awaited the Guides on their return from Delhi. Within two months they were again taking the field, under Sir Sidney Cotton, against the Hindustani fanatics of Sittana.

These fanatics, as they were called, were really refugees from British territory, for the most part deserters from corps that had mutinied, or outlaws who had participated in some unforgivable outrage; some, however, were clean-handed patriots, who, on principle, refused to bow to the decree of destiny, or to become peaceful subjects of the Queen. If the latter had remained quiet and inoffensive members of tribes or communities beyond our borders, the British Government, never vindictive, would probably, as the heat and passions of a desperate war died down, have left them to their solitude. But instead of thus living peaceably in the asylum they had found, they set about inciting their hot-blooded neighbours to join them in disturbing the peace of the border. They harried villages, drove off cattle, killed and wounded British subjects, and thus became an additional disturbing feature on a frontier always ready enough for the pleasure of a good fight. The opportunity was therefore taken of the presence of Sir Sidney Cotton's column to make them feel that the strong hand of the British Government could reach them even in their mountain fastnesses.

With the co-operation of a force from the Hazara district Sittana, the stronghold of the Hindustanis, was skilfully surrounded, and a fierce hand-to-hand conflict ensued. Their Pathan allies, whose hearts were evidently not in the business, showed but lukewarm enthusiasm, and escaped as best they could; but the Hindustanis stood to a man. They fought like fanatics, coming boldly and doggedly on, and going through all the preliminary attitudes and posturing of the Indian prize-ring. Their advance was made steadily and in perfect silence, without a shout or a word of any kind, unlike the yelling charge of the Afghan ghazi. All were dressed in their bravest and best for the occasion, as is meet for him who goes to meet his Lord, most of them in pure white, but some of the leaders in richly embroidered velvet coats. The fight was short, desperate, and decisive; and in the end every one of these brave, if misguided, warriors was killed or captured. The brunt of the charge fell on the 18th Punjab Infantry, who lost one officer and sixteen men in the encounter.

Many another fight too did the Guides have during the next few years with unvarying success, but we may perhaps pass the less important by, and come to the stiff encounter that faced them during the expedition against the Mahsud Waziri tribe in 1860.

The British force operating in that country had in the course of the campaign been split up into two columns; one under Sir Neville Chamberlain[12] had gone forward, lightly equipped, into the Waziri fastnesses; while a weaker column, some one thousand five hundred strong under Lumsden and including the Guides, was left at Pallosin to guard camp, equipage, and stores. Knowing the enemy he had to deal with, and his predilection for, and skill in executing the unexpected in war, Lumsden drew in his camp, so as to make it as snug and defensible as possible, and putting out strong picquets with their supports all round, he awaited the few days' absence of the main column. During the interval no

---
12. Afterwards Field-Marshal Sir Neville Chamberlain, G.C.B., &c.

signs of the enemy could be seen, nor could any news of him be obtained by means of spies. To all intents and purposes he seemed to have disappeared, and the little column lay, apparently unnoticed and unheeded, amidst the great mountains. Yet suddenly, from anywhere, from nowhere, from the very bowels of the earth, the Waziris rose in their thousands, and hurled themselves at the British camp.

Réveille was just sounding in the grey dawn of April 23rd, when three thousand Waziris armed with swords and guns, and fired with fierce fanaticism, boldly charged that side of the camp which was held by the Guides. The storm first fell on the outlying picquets, who fired a volley, and then received the great rush of white-robed swordsmen on their bayonets. They fought with the utmost gallantry, but the weight of numbers was against them, and in a few minutes, standing bravely at their posts, they were practically annihilated. Yet the strife was not in vain, for it was strong enough to cause all but the bravest of the brave to pause before proceeding to attack the kernel of the nut, whose shell had been so hard to crack. And thus it came about that only five hundred of the three thousand swordsmen faced the death beyond. These, with scarce a pause, and calling loudly on Allah to give them victory, swept swiftly on to the camp of the Guides. In that war-seasoned corps, half an hour before dawn, wet or dry, in freezing cold or tropical heat, the inlying picquet, a hundred strong, falls in, and stands silent, fully equipped, armed, and ready for all emergencies, till broad daylight shows all clear and safe. At the first sound of the firing Lumsden jumped to his feet, and taking this inlying picquet, rushed out of camp at its head, and so posted it as to enfilade and hold in check the great body of Waziris who now darkened the skyline. Then, hastening back to camp, he reached it almost abreast of the five hundred, who were not to be denied.

Now commenced the very babel of conflict; horses and

A NON-COMMISSIONED OFFICER OF THE GUIDES' INFANTRY

mules neighing and screaming and straining at their ropes, dogs barking, men yelling, the clash of swords, the rattle and crash of musketry, the screams of the wounded and the groans of the dying. Was ever such a pandemonium? The Guides in small knots, though hard stricken, fought with determined courage; but they were gradually driven back, inch by inch, till they were almost on to the guns parked in the rear. Then came to the rescue the keen resource and ready courage of the British subaltern. Borne back in the rush were Lieutenants Bond and Lewis of the Guides; but in the awful din and confusion they could at first do little else but defend themselves. Gradually, however, they formed the few men near them into a rough line, and by dint of shouting and passing the word along, succeeded in getting more men to catch the notion; till in a few minutes they had the best part of two hundred men in line right across the camp. Then came the order passed along with a roar, "Fix bayonets!" This order was in fact superfluous, for every man was already busy holding his own with his bayonet; but there is a certain sequence in military orders, which in times of confusion tend to steady the nerves with the cool touch of drill and discipline. The sequence of the order "Fix bayonets!" is "Charge!" When that sequence came a wild cheer echoed down the line of the Guides; as one man they leaped forward, and with thrust and staggering blow cleared the camp of the enemy. As they retreated the 4th Sikhs and 5th Gurkhas took them in flank, and in a few minutes turned a repulse into a headlong flight. The enemy left one hundred and thirty-two dead on the ground, ninety-two of whom were in the Guides' camp, and carried off immense numbers of wounded and dying. The Guides lost thirty-three killed and seventy-four wounded.

This was Lumsden's last fight at the head of the Guides. Now a Lieutenant-Colonel and a Companion of the Bath, his promotion was assured, and it came with his transfer to the command of the Hyderabad contingent, with the rank of Brigadier-General. This fine soldier from the raising of the corps in 1846 had held command of it for sixteen years; the brightest example of what a brave, chivalrous, and resourceful leader should be. Commanders of regiments come and go, and few leave their mark; but over the Guides the influence of Lumsden still burns bright and clear. To be alert and ready; to rise equal to the occasion, be the call small or great; to be not easily taken aback in a sudden emergency; to be a genial comrade and a good sportsman,--such are the simple soldier maxims left to his comrades by one of the best soldiers who ever drew sword.

The extraordinary devotion felt for Lumsden by the rude warriors whom he had enlisted and trained to war was somewhat pathetically, if quaintly, illustrated by an incident that occurred not long before he left. Sir John Lawrence, then Lieutenant-Governor of the Punjab, had been round to inspect the Guides, for in those days they were not under the orders of the Commander-in-Chief, but directly under the Civil Government. Something in the course of the day had occurred to put Sir John Lawrence out of humour, and he was at all times a man of blunt speech. Whatever it was, it temporarily annoyed Lumsden, and quite unwittingly this became evident to the faithful fellows who were ready to charge into hell-fire at his order. It was a mere passing cloud, for the cheery bright-hearted Lumsden was no man to brood over small matters of this sort. As, however, he sat out under the stars smoking his last pipe, he became aware of a figure in the background, and turning round saw one of his orderlies respectfully standing at attention.

"Hullo! What's up?" asked Lumsden.

"It is only this," replied the orderly, one of the rough warriors who took orders only from his own sahibs, and cared not a jot for any other man, black or white. "It is only this, Sahib: I and my comrades noticed that the Lord Sahib spoke to-day words that were not pleasing to your Excellency, and that you were angry and displeased when you heard them. So we have consulted together as to how best we may serve the proper end; for it is not right and proper that we should allow our Colonel Sahib to be harshly spoken to by anyone. There is, therefore, this alternative: the Lord Sahib has arranged to leave by the straight road to-morrow morning for Peshawur, but with your honour's kind permission, and by the Grace of God, there is no reason whatever why he should ever reach it." That man thoroughly meant what he said, and to this day the same touching devotion of the men to their officers, though perhaps less bluntly expressed, is still one of the characteristics of the Guides.

Many years afterwards Lord William Beresford, when Military Secretary to the Viceroy, was fond of telling a story not only illustrative of the personal equation which would cause one of the rough and ready old soldiers to refuse obedience to any but his own officers, but also giving a somewhat embarrassing illustration of a sentry adhering too literally to his orders. Lord William was somewhat annoyed at the time; but when cooler, he saw the sound military spirit underlying the incident, and hence always mentioned it with commendation.

It appears that as the Guides' cavalry were marching in to Rawul Pindi for a concentration of troops, just before they reached their camping-ground they passed a pond by the roadside. The officer commanding turning round, called one of the men to him and said: "Go, stand sentry on that pond, and don't let anyone water there, till we have watered our horses."

"Very good, your Honour," replied the trooper, and went and posted himself.

What the commanding officer really meant was, not to allow cattle and transport animals to dirty the water before the horses came down to drink; but he did not express himself very clearly.

Shortly after the sentry had taken up his beat a string of horses, headed by a gorgeous being in a scarlet uniform, appeared, making for the pond.

"Hullo! you there, where are you going?" shouted the sentry.

"Going?" repeated the gorgeous being, superciliously. "Why, to water my horses, you stupid fool."

"No you don't," said the sentry; "no one waters here till the Guides have finished with it."

The gorgeous person nearly fell off his horse with astonishment, and when he found speech he replied: "Cease prattling, son of an impure mother! These are the Great Lord's horses, and can of course water where and when they choose."

"I don't care a quarter of an anna whose horses they are, but they don't water here. So, out of this, you mis-begotten son of a red-coated ape, or I'll give you something to help you along." And the sentry quietly pulled out a cartridge, and began leisurely fitting it into the breech of his carbine.

This was not at all to the red-coated gentleman's liking. To trot behind his Lord, richly caparisoned and splendidly mounted, was one thing; but to meet an infernal fellow who deliberately fitted a cartridge into his carbine to defend his post, was a matter not lightly to be undertaken. Accordingly he galloped off to fetch his native officer. When this officer arrived he was much enraged, and roundly abused the sentry, calling him every name under the sun, and casting the gravest reflections on the whole of his ancestors, especially on the female side.

But the sentry stood like a block of wood, and when the other had finished answered: "I don't know who you are, and don't care; and for the present you may talk as much as you like, though when I am at liberty I also shall have a few words to say. But I am sentry here on this pond, and my orders are such and such, and I mean to obey them. The first man who tries to force me I hit with a bullet."

"Was there ever such a person?" said the native officer. "He must be mad! And the Great Lord's horses too! God preserve him; he will certainly be hanged, or sent across the Black Water for life."

So he too rode off to fetch his sahib; and shortly a trail of dust on the road showed that he was returning, and not leisurely. The officer was hot, indignant, and vexed, and said to the sentry: "By my order you will allow the Viceroy's horses to water at this pond."

"With every respect," replied the sentry, "my own Sahib has given me other orders, and I mean to obey him."

And nothing the officer could say, and he said a good deal, could move the sentry one hair'sbreadth from that resolve. So he, in his turn, rode off to fetch the last court of appeal, the Military Secretary, Lord William Beresford.

As all who knew him will remember, his Lordship was very short and sharp when anything occurred that in the least infringed the dignity of the Viceroy, or of anything belonging to that exalted personage; and probably few would have cared to be in the shoes of that sentry during the next few minutes. But the sentry was sublimely oblivious of the existence of so high an official as a Military Secretary, and only dimly aware of the existence of a Great Lord. On the other hand his own Colonel Sahib and his own sahibs, with whom he had fought and bled, were real live people, whom he knew quite well and whose word was law unto him. The Military Secretary, therefore, being evidently an older and more worthy sahib than the last, was received with even more respect; but as to allowing the horses to water, the sentry was adamant on that point. "I obey my

Colonel's orders," said he, "and no one else's." Lord William, though greatly vexed, as perhaps was only natural, was too good a soldier to force a sentry, and rode off therefore to the Guides' camp to lay the matter before the commanding officer. The rest was naturally all cordiality and good feeling, and an invitation to lunch; while the Guides' subaltern galloped off and cut the Gordian knot.

Scarcely had Lumsden parted from his beloved corps, when they again took the field, in the small but bloody Umbeyla campaign of 1863. The opening incident was in what was coming to be honourably looked upon as thoroughly Guides' fashion. Two troops of the cavalry and two companies of the infantry of this corps, under Jenkins,[13] were encamped at Topi, blockading the Gaduns and Hindustani fanatics preparatory to the advance of the field-force. One night a patrol of three men, under Duffadar Fakira, suddenly encountered a body of about three hundred of the enemy, on their way to surprise and capture the camp of the Guides. Without a moment's hesitation, and with highly commendable presence of mind, the duffadar began shouting "Fall in! fall in!" as if addressing countless legions; and then wheeling his three men into line, and each man yelling like a dozen fiends, fell with fury on the advancing enemy. The effect was magical, the enemy thinking that they had been betrayed, or forestalled, or had perchance fallen into an ambush, and that opposed to them was the whole strength of the Guides. In the darkness a panic set in, and the whole force broke and fled, their redoubted and sainted leader, the Mullah Abdullah, showing the way.

In the fierce and frequent fighting which week after week, raged round the celebrated Crag picquet, the Guides took their part. This picquet stood at the top of an abrupt and precipitous rock, accessible from our side only by a narrow rocky path, while towards the enemy the ground

---

13. Afterwards Colonel Sir Francis Jenkins, K.C.B.

sloped away to further hills. The weakness of the picquet, therefore, lay not only in its openness to determined attack, in days of short-range weapons and hand-to-hand fighting, but also in the difficulty experienced in quickly reinforcing it. Once taken, not only the neighbouring post, known as the Monastery picquet, but the whole camp lay under its commanding fire.

The first occasion on which the Crag was seriously attacked was before dawn on the 30th of October, when the picquet was rushed, and the twelve men of the 1st Punjab Infantry who held it were swept from the crest, but like limpets bravely clung to the near slopes. In support, close below, lay Major Keyes[14] with the remainder of the 1st Punjab Infantry and a company of the Guides. Owing to the rocky and difficult ascent it was impossible to do much till daylight, but with the first streak of dawn, valuably aided by the flank fire of Major Brownlow[15] and the 20th Punjab Infantry, Keyes himself at the head of the storming party most gallantly recaptured the Crag picquet at the point of the bayonet. As illustrating the severity of this hand-to-hand fighting, it may be mentioned that the enemy left sixty dead or dying, mostly Hindustani fanatics, in and round the picquet, while our own losses amounted to fifty-five.

In this gallant assault the company of the Guides bore their share, and four of them are mentioned as having been amongst the first into the recaptured position. The next serious assault took place on November the 12th, but after severe fighting was beaten off by Major Brownlow and the 20th Punjab Infantry, again supported by two companies of the Guides. A native officer of the Guides was specially mentioned on this occasion for carrying

---

14. Afterwards Commandant of the Guides and later General Sir Charles Keyes, K.C.B., etc.
15. Afterwards General Sir Charles Brownlow, G.C.B., etc.

ammunition at great personal risk up to the besieged picquet. It was estimated that two thousand of the enemy took part in this assault.

The third assault on this historic picquet was made by the undaunted tribesmen on November the 13th, when it was held by the 1st Punjab Infantry; and so determined and strongly supported was the attack that not only was the picquet, now one hundred and twenty strong, driven off the hill, but something like a panic spread amongst the followers in camp, much disturbing the dispositions made for recapturing the Crag. The first attempt to stem the tide was made by detachments of the Guides and 1st Punjab Infantry, but these were not strong enough to retake the picquet, and could barely hold their own. Then came to the rescue Major C.C.G. Ross with detachments of the Guides, 1st Punjab Infantry, and 14th Native Infantry, which, charging up, got close to the crest, but were not strong enough to drive out the swarms of determined warriors grimly holding the vantage ground.

The matter had now reached a serious point, at once apparent to Sir Neville Chamberlain; for the possession of the Crag picquet by the enemy made untenable the whole British position. He therefore immediately ordered to the assault the 101st Royal Bengal Fusiliers.[16] This gallant regiment aided by three companies of the Guides, and the line swelled by Major Ross's mixed detachments, without a check stormed and captured the position with the bayonet. The enemy lost two hundred and thirty men in this gallant attempt, while our own casualties reached one hundred and fifty-eight.

The final attempt came on the afternoon of November the 20th. The post was then garrisoned by one hundred bayonets of the 101st Royal Bengal Fusiliers and one hundred bayonets of the 20th Punjab Infantry. Again so

---

16. Now the Royal Munster Fusiliers.

determined was the attack, and made in such strength, that the British garrison was swept from the hill with considerable loss. The position of affairs was now so critical that Sir Neville Chamberlain himself determined to lead the columns detailed to assault and retake the picquet. In this fine advance the 71st Highland Light Infantry, supported by the Guides, made the frontal attack, and so impetuous was their charge that the summit was reached and the enemy driven from it with little loss. Our total casualties in the affair, however, reached one hundred and fifty-three, while the estimated loss of the enemy was three hundred and twenty.

Such was the history of the Crag picquet, four times fiercely attacked with overwhelming numbers by a brave and fanatical foe, thrice captured, and thrice by sterling grit and stout endeavour bravely recaptured. Of a surety this bloody site has earned the title given it by all the countryside. It is called the Kutlgar, or the Place of Slaughter, for of friend and foe well nigh a thousand warriors had shed their blood to keep or take that barren rock.

Eight of the Guides received the Indian soldiers' highest reward for conspicuous gallantry in the field during these strenuous assaults and counter assaults.

Though this was no cavalry country, as may readily be judged, several troops of the Guides' cavalry, together with the 11th Bengal Cavalry, did useful service on more than one occasion, under the gallant leadership of Colonel Dighton Probyn,[17] one of the brilliant band of cavalry soldiers who had earned undying fame in the great Mutiny. It is perhaps the memory of those old days of dangers and troubles passed through together, that keeps alive the kindly feeling which leads Sir Dighton Probyn to write a few words of brave encouragement when his old comrades

---

17. Later the Right Honourable Sir Dighton Probyn, V.C., G.C.B., G.C.S.I., G.C.V.O., P.C., etc. etc., Keeper of the Privy Purse.

of the Guides take their share of such fighting as still, from time to time, falls to their lot. On their side the Guides look on him, along with Lumsden and Jenkins and other old heroes, as one of their own sahibs.

The element of secrecy is absolutely essential to a successful surprise. This is a military truism all the world over, but applies with special force amongst the Pathan tribes on the North-West Frontier of India, as indeed it did amongst the Boers, and for probably a very similar reason. They were not always professional spies whom the Boers employed; nor is it always a Pathan spy who is on the spot. But both peoples without having any highly organised system have been exceedingly fortunate in the manner in which information of impending movements has somehow got reported in the nick of time in the most interesting quarter.

Due south from Mardan, and distant, as the crow flies, some thirty-five to forty miles, lies the village of Paia, which for high crimes and misdemeanours, including murder, rapine, and arson, it was considered necessary to punish. Now punishment in the days of Cavignari not unusually meant waking up some fine morning to find that before breakfast it was either necessary to meet the Guides in a pitched battle, or to submit quietly to the demands of Government, and expiate the crimes committed. The difficulty, from our point of view, was to place the troops in the desired position, at the desired moment, without previously informing the enemy of the proposal. Failing this, either an ambush would be prepared into which the troops might fall, thus reversing the tables; or the whole village, men, women, and children, flocks and herds, and all the chickens that could be caught on short notice, would migrate bodily for a few days, till the storm was overpast. Then they would quietly return and cheerfully resume the uneven tenor of their ways.

AN AFRIDI OF THE GUIDES' INFANTRY

Now Paia was inhabited by Jowaki Afridis, and he that findeth an Afridi asleep, when he ought to be awake, is either a very astute or a very fortunate person. Cavignari was a very astute person and a match for the most wakeful Afridi. For instance, the British troops that lay nearest to Paia were those in garrison at Nowshera, and these, therefore, were the most obvious ones to use. Being the most obvious, it was at once decided that they were not the troops to use. Therefore Cavignari refrained from touching the Nowshera garrison, and called on the Guides, who were sixteen miles further away, and watching quite another frontier, to undertake the business.

But here again a difficulty arose; the Guides on their way would have to pass through Nowshera, and as that place was doubtless full of spies, no better result could be hoped for than by using a Nowshera regiment direct. And there was yet another difficulty: it was the middle of the hot weather and a great many of the British officers of the Guides, including the Commanding Officer, were away on leave; to recall them was to make the ears prick up of every person, with a guilty conscience, within a fifty mile radius.

But after all, military difficulties are possibly only introduced by a beneficent Providence lest warlike operations should become too easy; at any rate these were in due course overcome, though it required considerable ingenuity to do so. In the first place the Guides were marched off, without a notion what they were required for, or whither they were going. All they knew was that they were plodding along the Nowshera road on a very hot evening in August. When well on their way, like a man-of-war at sea they opened their sealed orders, and learnt that in the vicinity of Nowshera they would find a fleet of boats on the Kabul River. Embarking on these they were to drop down that river, now in flood, to its confluence with the Indus at Attock. Here the flotilla was to be concealed while one or two intelligent men were sent ashore to a place of tryst, whither Major R.B. Campbell, the Commanding Officer, and the other officers on leave, had been ordered to arrive by a certain hour. Then, complete in officers, the flotilla was to slip anchor again and drop down the roaring flood of the Indus for another twenty-eight miles to Shadipore, the local Gretna Green, to judge from its name. It speaks highly for the skill with which the operation was planned, and the exactitude with which it was executed, to record that it was carried out without a hitch. The Guides by a seventy-eight mile circuit now found themselves south-east, instead of north, of the objective, and the enemy were consequently taken from a totally unexpected quarter.

Another of Cavignari's coups may perhaps be given as illustrating not only his policy of smiting hard, instead of palavering, but also the necessity for strict secrecy. In 1878 when the Swat River Canal, which has turned the desert plain of Yusufzai into one great wheat-field, was under construction, the more pestilential class of mullah, always on the look-out for a cause to inflame Mahomedan fanaticism against the English unbeliever, stirred up the tribesmen to interfere with the work. A raid was consequently made by them, and a lot of harmless coolies murdered. The village of Sapri, just across the border, was chiefly implicated in this outrage, and Cavignari immediately demanded the surrender of the murderers, as well as a heavy fine in money wherewith to pension the families of the victims. Secure in their fastness the men of Sapri sent replies, varying from the evasive to the impertinent.

Cavignari said nothing more, but secretly warned the Guides, who lay forty-three miles away, to be ready to act. So carefully was the news kept that a movement was on foot, that some of the officers were playing racquets up to the last moment, and were called from the court to march at once. Captain Wigram Battye was in command, and took with him the Guides' cavalry and a detachment of Guides' infantry mounted on mules. Marching all night, the force arrived three miles beyond Abazai and within eight miles of its objective, when it was found impossible, owing to the difficult nature of the country, to proceed further on horseback. All the horses were consequently sent back to Fort Abazai, and the dismounted cavalry and infantry went on in the darkness over a most stony precipitous country. By strenuous effort the village of Sapri was reached and surrounded by daybreak. The villagers immediately rushed to arms and prepared for a desperate resistance, but the Guides were not to be denied; they carried the place, killing many and capturing the ringleaders, and nine others of those implicated in the murders. Our own losses were eight men wounded; while two received the Order of Merit for conspicuous bravery in action.

Such were a few of the adventures of the Guides during the twenty years which elapsed between the Mutiny and the Afghan War.

## Chapter 8
# The Massacre of the Guides at Kabul, 1879

The annals of no army and no regiment can show a brighter record of devoted bravery than has been achieved by this small band of Guides. By their deeds they have conferred undying honour, not only on the regiment to which they belong, but on the whole British Army.... The conduct of the escort of the Queen's Own Corps of Guides does not form part of the enquiry entrusted to the Commission, but they have in the course of their enquiries had the extreme gallantry of the bearing of these men so forcibly brought to their notice that they cannot refrain from placing on record their humble tribute of admiration.

So wrote the brave, bluff soldier, Sir Charles Macgregor, as president of the Committee appointed to enquire into the causes of the dreadful tragedy which in a few hours ended in the massacre of Sir Louis Cavignari and the whole of his escort.

When Cavignari, as minister and plenipotentiary on behalf of the British Government, signed the treaty of Gundamuk, one of the provisions of which was that a British Embassy with a suitable escort should be established at Kabul, there were many who, unable to forget the long-drawn history of Afghan treachery, looked with grave apprehension on the proposal. The Amir Yakub Khan, himself but lately and unsecurely seated on the throne, was not strong enough, it was urged, to uphold this new departure, even were he honestly anxious to do so. But against all opposition Cavignari placed his commanding personality and strong prevailing will; and by degrees he calmed not only any doubts the Amir on the one hand may have expressed, but on the other removed by convincing argument the objections raised by the prophets of evil in our own camp. Finally, to prove his unwavering confidence in the practicability of establishing a British Embassy at Kabul, he asked to be allowed in his own person to prove the soundness and safety of the policy he advocated.

The treaty of Gundamuk was signed in June 1879; but the Amir asked for a short respite, that he might return to his capital to prepare quarters for the Embassy and also accustom the minds of his people to its proposed arrival. It was not therefore till July 24th that Sir Louis Cavignari and his escort arrived at Kabul.

This escort consisted of twenty-five, of all ranks, of the Guides' cavalry, and fifty-two, of all ranks, of the Guides' infantry under the command of Lieutenant Walter Hamilton, who a few weeks before had won the Victoria Cross at the action of Fattehabad The other Englishmen with the Embassy were Surgeon A.H. Kelly of the Guides, as medical officer, and Mr. W. Jenkins, as political assistant to Sir Louis Cavignari.

The reception of the Embassy at Kabul was to all seeming perfectly friendly, and even cordial. Every honour was paid to it, and the assembled crowds, though preserving the impassive mien of Asiatics on such occasions, respectfully saluted the British officers as they passed along. It had been arranged that the members of the Embassy and escort should take up their abode in quarters prepared for them in the Bala Hissar, the celebrated fortress which is indelibly connected with the name of Kabul, and which completely dominates the city. Here also were the Amir's palace and the houses of many of his highest nobles.

For a month all went well. Cavignari paid frequent visits to the Amir, and entered into long and friendly converse with him. The Amir's nobles and officials paid frequent return visits of ceremony or friendship. The officers of the Embassy rode out daily, morning and evening, to see the country and surrounding places of interest, accompanied always, however, by escorts of Afghan cavalry as well as of the Guides. To encourage friendly intercourse, they used to practise tent-pegging and lime-cutting, and invited the Afghan horsemen to join them. But, as showing how curious are the workings of the Asiatic mind, it afterwards transpired that this apparently unexceptional proceeding was looked on by many with grave offence. The Afghan officers muttered that this was mere braggadocio on the part of the sahibs; that the sport was only to show how they would spit and cut down the sons of the Prophet, if they had the chance! To fathom such depths of bigotry as this incident reveals is one of the many difficulties which face Englishmen in Asia.

Towards the end of August Sir Louis Cavignari received one or two direct warnings that all was not well. It appears that in the ordinary course of the relief of various garrisons several of the Amir's Herati regiments were ordered from Herat to Kabul, and Kabul regiments took their place. These Herati regiments had seen nothing of the late war: they had never crossed swords with the British; and they were filled with the insensate pride and confidence in their own prowess which abysmal ignorance could alone account for. As they marched through the streets of Kabul they set up, at the instigation of their officers it is said, loud cries of insult and abuse of Cavignari by name, of the British Embassy, and of the whole detested race of Feringhis. When this was told to Cavignari he merely laughed and replied: "Curs only bark, they do not bite." In a broad sense he was right, for if British officers had always lain down wherever stray curs were moved to yelp, the British Empire's outer frontier of to-day would be the cliffs of Dover. But a much more weighty warning came from an undoubted well-wisher, an old retired native officer of our Indian army, and a firm friend of the envoy. His warning said that a plot was afoot; that the cupidity of some had been appealed to by stories of large treasure in the Residency, while the fanatical hatred of others had been secretly fanned; that it was well therefore to be on guard. A warning coming from such a friendly quarter was doubtless duly weighed and duly allowed for; but after all, what could a peaceful Embassy do but trust to the honour and integrity of the friendly Power whose guest it was? To show the smallest sign of distrust by attempting, for instance, to place a merely residential set of buildings, completely commanded all round, into a state of defence, was only to court disaster. What could the British Ambassador in Paris do against a brigade of troops unrestrained by the French Government? What could an escort of seventy-five men, however brave, do against thousands, and tens of thousands, of armed men? Cavignari therefore took the bold course, which British officers, before and since, have taken. He sat quietly, and with good and brave heart faced the coming storm, if come it must; but greatly confident that it might split and roll by on either side.

In the end, by sad mischance, a small matter, and one quite unconnected, directly or indirectly, with the attitude of the British Embassy, caused the storm to burst with sudden and uncontrollable fierceness. The already half-mutinous Herati regiments were, as was not unusual in those days, very much in arrears as regards their pay. For months they had received none, and were, perhaps naturally, in an angry and sullen mood. The finances of the State were in a chaotic condition, the treasury at low ebb, and credit had receded to a vanishing point. After staving off the day of reckoning as long as possible, the welcome news reached the Herati troops that they were to receive their pay in full next morning, September 3rd, at the treasury in the Bala Hissar.

Assembling there early, they soon learnt to their disgust and indignation that they were only to receive one month's pay, a miserable pittance to men long in want. On the smouldering embers of mutiny someone wilfully, or from mere expediency, threw the spark: "Go to the British Embassy and demand pay; there is lots of money there." The idea caught like wildfire, and the whole mass of soldiery dashed off to the Embassy, situated only a few hundred yards away.

Here the ordinary routine of the day was going on. It was eight o'clock, and Cavignari, just returned from his morning ride, had not yet bathed or changed for breakfast. Hamilton and Kelly had been out to see that the grass-cutters were at their work on waste land, and not interfering with private rights, and were now probably strolling down the line of troop-horses seeing to their feeding and grooming. Jenkyns was doubtless within, reading or writing, and waiting for breakfast. The cavalrymen were about amongst their horses, and the infantry either on guard or taking their ease. On this peaceful scene suddenly burst a torrent of infuriated, half-savage soldiery, yelling for Cavignari, yelling for money, shouting curses and threats. At first they acted like mere Yahoos; they hustled and mobbed the Guides, shouting with rough humour, "Well, if we can't get money we'll get something," and then began untying horses to lead them away, stealing saddlery, swords, or anything that lay about. Then came a shot and silence; then another and another, five or six in all, by whom fired no one knows; and then the battle began,--four British officers and some seventy of the Guides, against countless thousands!

Nor was the vantage of position with the British, for they could not possibly have been more unfavourably situated for defence. The Residency consisted of a collection of mud and plaster buildings, of which the principal was the abode of the British officers. The others included the rows

The Memorial Arch and Tank to the memory of Sir Louis Cavignari and the officers and non-commissioned officers and men of the Guides killed in the defence of the Kabul Residency, September 3, 1879. In the foreground is a brass cannon captured during the Relief of Chitral

of huts that formed the barracks of the escort, servants' houses, and stables; outside, and enclosed by mud walls, were spaces in which were picketed the horses of the cavalry, and which formed courtyards to the Residency and men's barracks. Residential quarters of this description, given time to loop-hole and barricade them, would form fairly good defensive cover, except against artillery; but unprepared for defence they are mere death-traps. To add to the untenable nature of the position the Residency was completely commanded from several directions, and especially from a high flat-roofed house only eighty yards distant. The roofs of the Residency buildings were also flat, but made untenable by these commanding positions, except in one small portion where a low parapet, such as is often found on Eastern roofs, gave some slight protection.

After those first few shots there seems to have been a pause, while the mutinous troops rushed off to their camp to fetch arms and ammunition. During this brief respite Cavignari sent a message to the Amir, who was in his palace only a few hundred yards distant, informing him of the unprovoked attack, and claiming the protection due to a guest of the nation; while Hamilton hastily collected his men, and made such dispositions for defence as were possible. Then above the dust and din and rush of hurrying feet outside rose, clearer and stronger as hundreds of throats joined the swelling sound, *Yar Charyar,* the war-cry of the great Sunni sect of Mahomedans. They were coming in their thousands frenzied with fanaticism, and thirsting deep for Christian blood. On the other side, in calm and steadfast readiness, stood three score and ten of the Guides, men of an alien race, and some even brethren of the besiegers, but all filled with high resolve and stern determination to stand by their British officers even unto death.

Sir Louis Cavignari, soldier when diplomacy ceased, was the first to seize a rifle, and, lying prone on the flat exposed roof, with quick precision, one after the other, shot dead four leaders of the assault. But raked as he was from the higher positions, a splintered bullet hit him in the forehead, and he had to be taken below to have his wound dressed. Yet undaunted, when the first shock passed, he must have risen again, for an eye-witness from a neighbouring house declares he saw four sahibs charge out at the head of their men, and one of these must have been Cavignari. And that was the last of the fight for that brave soul, for the only further glimpse was that of a hurrying soldier, who saw him laid on a bed, with his feet drawn up, his hand to his head, and the doctor at his side.

This was all early in the day, perhaps before ten o'clock, and from this time forth the whole burden of defence lay on a young subaltern of the Guides, Walter Hamilton. Yet he was not alone, for sharing his glorious toil, and rising to the heights of heroism, was Jenkyns, a man of peace, bred not to war or the sword, and Kelly, physician and healer, but no fighting man.

And now in addition to the heavy fire from the house-tops the mutineers bored loop-holes through the compound walls, and through these, themselves protected, poured a murderous fire into the devoted building. Covered by this fire, escalading ladders were run forward at a dead angle, and in a moment the roof was reached, and the small remnant of Guides, six or seven in all, still manning the little parapet were driven below. After them, gallantly enough, the besiegers rushed down the steps; but there they met their fate, for, turning fiercely on them, the Guides killed many, and drove the survivors back to the roof. It was at this time that the first signs of fire were noticed, whether intentionally ignited by the storming party, or accidental, is not clear, though later conflagrations were undoubtedly intentional.

But though the fight had now waxed stronger and

STATUE OF LIEUTENANT WALTER HAMILTON,
ERECTED IN DUBLIN MUSEUM

stronger for five hours, and though nearly one-half of the garrison were killed or wounded, though the British Envoy lay dead or dying, no thought of surrender occurred to the stout hearts within. Only, for the third time that morning, was an attempt made by letter to remind the Amir of his sacred obligations as a host and sovereign of a friendly Power. On this occasion the bearer selected was Shahzada Taimus, a Prince of the Sadozai dynasty, but a plain trooper in the ranks of the Guides' cavalry. The two preceding letters had been sent, one by the hand of an old pensioner of the Guides, slipped through an unguarded postern, but not seen again and supposed to be killed; and the second by a Hindu, who was indeed killed before the eyes of the garrison in his brave attempt to get through.

The third letter was written by Mr. Jenkyns, and handed by Hamilton to the Shahzada, a quiet unassuming man, to take to the Amir. A forlorn hope indeed faced the brave fellow, as he looked forth through a crevice at the yelling, shooting, cursing crowd, surging round on all sides. To open a door was instant death to himself and others, for a shower of bullets would have greeted his exit. The postern was now surrounded, and gave no hope of escape. There remained only the roof, and this means of escape Taimus decided to attempt. Crawling cautiously up, he found this bullet-swept area temporarily deserted, and creeping along it peered over the end. There he saw, only some ten feet beneath him, a furious crowd, many hundreds strong, and those nearest the wall busy digging a hole through it into the building.

Well, if he had to die, it was the will of God; he would fight his way through, or fall sword in hand. Standing up in full view, for a second the observed of all observers, armed to the teeth, he calmly jumped into the jaws of those baying wolves. The shock of the fall was unwillingly broken by the astonished forms of those on whom he fell, and before they could grapple with him he was pushing boldly through the crowd. But the odds and press were too great for him, and after a brief close scuffle he was for want of elbow-room overpowered and disarmed. Many shouted "Kill him! Kill him! he is a Cavignari-ite!" But above the uproar, holding his hands above his head, Taimus made himself heard. "Peace! peace!" he cried. "I undoubtedly eat the salt of the Sirkar, but I am alone and disarmed, a Mahomedan amongst Mahomedans, and the bearer of a letter to the Amir. Kill me if you like, but yours be the shame and disgrace." As he spoke, amidst the crowd of angry, scowling faces he saw a friend, a man of influence and standing; at his word the crowd gave way, and battered, bleeding, and closely guarded, Taimus was taken before the Chief. But help was now out of the Amir's power, as he sat bemoaning his fate in the women's apartments. He could give no succour he said, but he gave orders for Taimus to be detained in a place of safety. To finish the story of Shahzada Taimus: while confined there a havildar of the mutineers was brought in with a bullet in his back, and in his agony he besought Taimus to extract it. This the Shahzada, though no surgeon, succeeded in doing with a pocket-knife, and so grateful was the mutineer that when night fell he gave him his uniform and helped him to escape; and eventually, after many adventures and by the use of many disguises, the brave fellow reached India in safety.

But to return to the Residency. Jemadar[18] Mehtab Sing, one of the two native officers of the Guides, was now dead, and Kelly's whole time was occupied in attending as best he could to the wounded, of whom there were now twenty or thirty. There remained in the fighting line only Hamilton, Jenkyns, Jemadar Jewand Sing, and some thirty of the Guides. The whole interior of the building was full of dead

---

18. Jemadar, a native commissioned officer, next in rank to the subadar.

and dying, enemies and friends, the atmosphere made still more oppressive by the smoke of powder, and by the more deadly peril of creeping incendiarism.

At this juncture, loud and exulting shouts proclaimed that fresh heart had been given to the besiegers by the arrival of some new reinforcement. The cause was self-apparent; two guns were being run by hand into position at the gateway barely one hundred yards away. Two guns, neither then nor now, could face the open within a hundred yards of armed infantry who could freely use their weapons. But here was a different case. Driven by the storm of fire all round into rooms without loopholes, and incapable of affording either offensive or defensive fire, the Guides could only get snapshots here and there as occasion offered.

By a curious coincidence the story of those newly-arrived guns was told with almost faithful accuracy, in the brief testimony of a witness who was nearly three miles away. He said: "We heard the big guns fire twice, and then there was silence for some time; then they fired once or twice more; and then, after a long interval, one or two more shots. Perchance, seven or eight shots altogether were fired." What to the distant hearer were impressive, unaccountable pauses, were on the scene of action filled with the bravest incidents. Cooped up as they were with a murderous artillery firing point blank into them at one hundred yards range, and spreading not only death and destruction amongst wounded and unwounded alike, but still further aiding the conflagration, which had by now taken well hold of the buildings, yet still stout of heart the Guides girded up their loins to meet the new encounter.

Dr. Kelly left his wounded, and Jenkyns, the young civilian, took again a sword and pistol, and with the boy Hamilton as their leader, and with twelve staunch and true men of the Guides behind them, they opened the door. Then charging forth, they quickly crossed the bullet-swept courtyard, and fell with fury on the amazed gunners and the crowd behind the wall. Shooting, thrusting, and slashing, they killed or routed every man about the guns, and seizing them tried to drag them back. But here their strength was too small, though great their heart, and though they swung the guns round, and pulled them a few yards, they could not get them away. The little band was falling fast, right out in the open as it was; and at last the overwhelming tide returned and drove them back with the loss of half their numbers. Dr. Kelly, too, must in the sortie have received his mortal wound, for though he struggled back with the rest, he was never again seen alive. *Requiescat in pace*: physician and soldier, he died a hero's death.

Again the furious crowd surged up to the guns, recaptured them, slewed them round, and laid them on the door. Then came the second salvo heard by the distant listener; and again, scarce taking breath, Hamilton made preparations for his new attempt. "Do you stand here and here; and you two, there and there; and all of you shoot for all you're worth at the gunners, while I and the rest again charge out and capture the guns," he said. "And I come too," said Jenkyns.

Then a second time they threw open the door, and a second time those two young Englishmen at the head of the faithful few charged out on the guns. But for Jenkyns the glorious end had come, and sword in hand he fell, some seventy paces out, a lasting honour to the great Civil Service of India. Yet on went Hamilton and his dwindling band, and taking no denial, stayed not by bullet nor sword nor bayonet, again captured the guns. And then began again the dreadful heart-straining struggle of desperate men set to a task too great. Again with splendid effort they dragged the guns a few yards, and again the great returning wave engulfed them, and fighting foot by foot the Guides were again driven back.

And now the flames had got strong hold of the buildings, and here and there the roofs fell in, and dead and dying were entombed together. So the few survivors driven from end to end found last refuge in the *hamam*, or bath, which, being below the surface of the ground and built of solid brick, gave welcome shelter. But even so death was but a question of hours or minutes, and neither Hamilton nor his men were of the sort to sit tamely down to wait for it. Taking rest for awhile from the exhaustion of seven hours of this Homeric struggle, the undefeated Hamilton again laid his plans. "Now two or three," said he, "will fire from here, so as to try to keep down the fire on our assaulting party, while the rest dash out again. Arrived at the guns, I alone will face the enemy, while all of you, paying no heed to the fighting, will harness yourselves to one gun and bring it in. We shall then, at least, have one gun less against us, and may perhaps be able to use the captured one in defence. Then, in the same way, we will again charge out, and get the other gun." "Your Honour speaks well, we are ready," said his men.

This was the fourth sortie Hamilton had led that day; the first with all four Englishmen in a line, the second with three, the third with two, and now alone. Over six feet in height, splendidly made, lithe and strong, with all the activity of youth, expert with sword and pistol, he was a noble specimen of the British officer, and none more fit than he to stand in the deadly breach. Out then they went and acted on the plan arranged. For a third time those fateful guns were captured, and then alone to stem the fierce assault stood Hamilton, while his men laboured at the gun; but the odds were too great, and the gallant subaltern, after killing three men with his pistol and cutting down two more with his sword, was himself borne down. And so fighting died as brave a young heart as ever did honour to the uniform he wore. Swarming over his body, the mutineers recaptured the gun and again drove back the remnants of the forlorn hope. Hamilton lay where he fell close to the gun, till darkening night settled down on the dreadful scene. But when, next morning, a witness passed that way, he mentions that the brave young fellow's body was laid across the gun. Perchance it was the kindly act of a friend, or perchance the rough chivalry of one who had watched his heroic deeds.

It might be thought that a day so full of great deeds, of patient courage, and unshaken loyalty could, as the sun sank slowly down, produce no further spark from those exhausted, starving few. But it remained for the evening hour to produce, perhaps, the brightest flash of all.

It was apparent to all the besiegers, fighters or spectators, that one by one all the sahibs had been killed or sore wounded, and that now none remained to lead their men. At intervals during the day loud voices, as of those in command, had shouted to the garrison of Guides: "We have no quarrel with you. Deliver over the sahibs, and you shall all go free, with what loot you can take. Be not foolish thus to fight for the cursed Feringhis against your own kith and kin." But for answer all they got was fierce showers of bullets, and fiercer still the staunch defenders cried: "Dogs and sons of dogs, is this the way you treat your nation's guests? To hell with you! we parley not with base-born churls!"

And now, again, when all the Englishmen were dead, the voices cried: "Why fight any longer? Your sahibs are killed. Save yourselves, and surrender, before you are all killed. We will give you quarter." Left in command was Jemadar Jewand Singh, a splendid Sikh officer of the Guides' cavalry, and not one whit behind his British officers in brave resolve. He designed no word of answer to the howling crowd without, but to the few brave survivors within, perhaps a dozen or so, he said: "The Sahibs gave us this duty to perform, to defend this Residency to the last. Shall we then disgrace the cloth we wear by disobeying their orders now they are dead? Shall we hand over the property of the Sirkar, and the dead bodies of our officers, to these sons of perdition? I for one prefer to die fighting for duty and the fame of the Guides, and they that will do likewise follow me." Then, as the evening closed, went forth unhurried the last slender forlorn hope. The light of the setting sun fell kindly on those grim and rugged faces, out of which all anger and excitement and passion had passed away: they were marching out to die, and they knew it. One last glimpse we have of their gallant end. From a window hard by an old soldier pensioner, himself a prisoner, saw, and bore witness, that the leader of those pathetic few, fighting with stern and steadfast courage, killed eight assailants before he himself, the last to fall, was overborne.

And so staunchly fighting they died to a man, that gallant group,--died to live for ever. But round them lay heaped six hundred dead, as silent witnesses of twelve hours' heroic fight. The night fell, and darkness and the silence of death succeeded the strife of a livelong summer's day.

With that wise statesmanship for which the British Government may claim its share, a national memorial was raised at Mardan to these deathless heroes, and on it is written: The annals of no army and no regiment can show a brighter record of devoted bravery than has been achieved by this small band of Guides.

Yet another scene in the tragedy remains to be told. It is a cold bleak day in early winter. On one side stand the blackened, bullet-riddled ruins of the Residency, much as we saw them last. To the left, drawn up as a guard, is a long double line of British soldiers with, bayonets fixed. Behind them, covering every coign of vantage, every roof and wall, are crowds of Afghans, silent, subdued, and expectant. In the centre, in an open space, stands a little group of British officers, one of whom holds a paper from which he reads. Facing the ruined Residency is a long grim row of gallows;

below these, bound hand and foot and closely guarded is a row of prisoners. A signal is given, and from every gibbet swings what lately was a man. These are the ringleaders in the insensate tragedy, who, brought to justice by the strong resistless power of British bayonets, hang facing the scene of their infamy, for a sign throughout the length and breadth of Asia of the righteous fate that overtakes those who disgrace the law of nations.

## Chapter 9
# The Afghan War, 1878 - 1880

The Afghan War of 1878-80 lives chiefly in the memory of all as connected with the rise to fame of one who has since earned a place in English history with Marlborough and Wellington. And coupled with his name remains indelibly engraved the great historic march from Kabul to Kandahar.

Though they took no part in that celebrated march, being so reduced in numbers by the stress of war after two years' arduous campaigning that fresh regiments took their place, yet the Guides look back with the greatest pride to having once served under Lord Roberts, and to having earned the kindly praise of this great Captain. To this day grey-bearded old warriors speak with quiet pride and affection of their fighting days with "Roberts Sahib" at Kabul; and many an old eye kindles and bent back straightens as they salute his picture in the mess. Some, too, will remember the exact place and date on which he shook hands with them, and congratulated them on some brave deed, as he pinned the star for valour on their breasts.

It is given to few men to gain the affection and soldierly respect of all, but Roberts possessed the two great merits in the eyes of the simple Indian soldier. He was always kind and considerate, though firm as a rock, and always brave: kind with the kindness which is never weary of watching over the welfare of all, never forgetting a friend however humble, and always remembering those little soldier courtesies which count for so much; brave not only with the bravery that wins the Victoria Cross, but which, stout of heart, looks clear and undaunted through the dark storm of a winter like that of 1879 at Kabul; and still burns bright when at seventy years of age he goes forth at his Queen's behest to turn back the dark tide of defeat in 1899, and bring back victory to her standards.

To give an instance of this magnetic influence,--one day long after the Afghan War, Lord Roberts, then Commander-in-Chief in India, was passing the camp of the Guides, riding quietly along, when the sentry on the quarter-guard, an old soldier, recognised him in the distance, and shouting as in duty bound, "Guard, turn out!" added unofficially, but louder still, "Roberts Sahib is coming." The words spread like lightning down the long lines of horses and rows of tents; and with one accord each man dropped his work at the magic name and dashed to the head of the camp to see their old leader and friend: it was no question of Commander-in-Chief, it was only their old comrade Roberts Sahib. Need it be recorded that when his old soldiers heard that in the day of trouble Lord Roberts had gone to South Africa, they remarked with quiet confidence, "Ah! now all will be well."

For the Guides, serving as part of the force under the command of the brave and chivalrous leader of light horse, Lt.-General Sir Sam Browne, K.C.B., V.C., the Afghan War opened with the operations resulting in the capture of the formidable fort of Ali Musjid, which bars the entrance to the far-famed Khyber Pass. Sir Sam Browne was an old Colonel of the Guides, and to meet again in the field was the meeting of old comrades and friends. Like Roberts, he knew how to use them, and how to get the best out of them; and the glowing words of his despatches show they served him well.

In the plan of operations for the capture of Ali Musjid one brigade was to attack in front, one in flank, and one by a wide détour through the mountains was to cut off the retreat. In this operation it fell to the Guides to accompany General Tytler's column, which was the one destined, after a long night march through the mountains, to drop down in rear of the fort. The column was greatly delayed owing to the difficulty of the country, great mountains of eight thousand feet high intervening; but Jenkins with the Guides and 1st Sikhs pushed on, and by their timely arrival broke the back of the desperate resistance met by the frontal attack. No Afghan or Pathan can stand the strain of being taken in rear; a *sauve qui peut* becomes at once the order of the day. Most of the enemy fled through the mountains, but a regiment of regular infantry took the road through the pass and was captured by Jenkins and his men. Next came a squadron of cavalry, and these bold fellows determined to make a dash for liberty. Scattering therefore and riding at a break-neck gallop many got through, though many lay dead and wounded on the ground; and then, out of the cloud of dust and smoke might be seen, calmly riding at a foot's pace, a solitary trooper. A perfect hailstorm of bullets was falling about him, not the tiny bullets we now use, but great one ounce Snyder bullets, such as would knock over an elephant; but though nearly eight hundred rifles were in action, the serene horseman appeared not the least discomposed, and except for a defiant wave of his sword he rode quietly on.

Then Jenkins, struck with the admiration of one brave man for another, sounded the cease fire; and in the dead stillness that followed the Colonel's orderly shouted down to the horseman to ask him who he was, and why he thus courted death. "Oh, brother," shouted the orderly, "who art thou and whence comest and whither goest?" "I am Bahaud-din Khan," replied the horseman, "and I come from Ali Musjid, which the Feringhis have taken, and I follow those sons of pigs, the Kasilbash Horse, who you saw pass in such a hurry just now."

"The Sahib says," shouted the orderly, "that surely you must be mad thus to walk your horse through a heavy fire like that."

"Not mad, tell the Sahib," replied the Afghan, "but fearing no man; and I shook my sword at you, and your hundreds of rifles, to show that I cared not that much for you."

"By Jove, he's a brave fellow!" said Jenkins; "tell him to come up and have a talk with me."

"By all means," was the cheery reply; and dismounting quietly, the man tied his horse to a bush, slipped his sword into its scabbard, and strolled up the hill.

"Well, now tell me all about yourself," was Jenkins's greeting.

"There is nothing much to tell. I live in Kabul and belong to the Kasilbash Horse, and my father was a soldier before me. But he was a brave fellow like myself; we are no mis-begotten apes, like those sons of perdition who fled just now. They are all cowards and runaways, and no fit company for a warrior."

Jenkins liked the look of the man, and his courage was beyond doubt, so he said cordially: "You're a fine fellow and I like you. Will you take on with the Guides?"

"Yes, I will," said the free-lance without a moment's hesitation.

So there and then, on the field of battle, Bahaud-din Khan, late of the Kasilbash Horse, joined the Guides, and was made a non-commissioned officer on the spot. For two long years, through the many ups and downs of the campaign, through much severe fighting and many a hardship, he did good and valiant service. It was only when the war was over, and the corps was nearing India on its downward march, that Bahaud-din Khan began to lose his reckless devil-may-care bearing; he seemed sad, and dispirited, and out of sorts altogether.

"Why, what ails you, my man?" said Jenkins one day as he chanced across him on the march.

"Nothing, Sahib; I am very happy in the service of the Queen, and I feel it an honour to serve in the Guides."

"Well, then, why look so doleful? One would think you

A Trooper of the Guides' Cavalry

had lost your best horse, or broken the sword of your ancestors on the head of a buffalo," laughed Jenkins.

"The truth cannot be hidden from you, Sahib, so I will tell it," ingenuously replied Bahaud-din Khan. "My comrades tell me that down at Mardan they have to do riding-school and drill, and all that sort of thing. Well, I don't think, Sahib, that is quite in my line. Give me as much fighting as you like, but I'm too old a soldier to go bumping round a riding-school. Therefore, with your Honour's kind permission I think I will take my leave, and return to Yaghistan, the land of never-ending conflict."

"By all means," said Jenkins; "no man stays in the Guides against his will. You are a free man from this moment."

And so, very near the same spot where he had taken service on the field of battle, Bahaud-din Khan quietly took his discharge, and rode off, like a knight of old, to place his sword at the service of any who wanted it. "But riding-school, God forbid!" he muttered as he went.

It is not intended to follow the Guides through all the phases of the Afghan War, but only to tell the story of some of their gallant adventures. One of the earliest of these was at the little battle of Fattehabad, where Wigram Battye was killed, and Walter Hamilton earned the Victoria Cross.[19] A small force consisting of portions of the 10th Hussars, Guides' cavalry, 17th Foot, forty-five Sikhs, together with a battery of horse-artillery, were sent on from Jellalabad, as an advance force to clear the road to Kabul. About twelve miles out, at the village of Fattehabad, General Gough[20] was suddenly threatened in flank by a great gathering of Afghan tribesmen.

Acting on the principle that in dealing with Asiatics it is always wise, whatever the odds, to attack, instead of waiting the onslaught, the General moved out rapidly with

---
19. Here again I have had to depart from strict chronology.
20. Afterwards General Sir Charles Gough, V.C., G.C.B., etc.

the cavalry and horse-artillery, and ordered the infantry to follow as quickly as possible. Getting in touch with the enemy, the horse-artillery came into action, but their fire, good and accurate as it might be, was not sufficient to stay the determined advance of large bodies of bloodthirsty and fanatical ghazis. The General, therefore, ordered the cavalry to charge, the two regiments acting independently under their own commanders.

Major Wigram Battye was commanding the squadron of the Guides' cavalry launched to the attack, but ere he had proceeded a few hundred yards a bullet hit him in the left hip, and the squadron, under Hamilton, swept on, leaving him still in the saddle, though in great pain and supported by his orderly.

Then happened one of those strange fatalities which brings the Kismet of the Mahomedan into close touch with the Providence of the Christian. Hamilton and the whole squadron galloping every second into more imminent danger remain unscathed. The solitary sore wounded horseman, walking his horse behind them, had that day come to the end of God's allotted span; and as he walked yet another chance bullet pierced his chest, and he fell to rise no more; the second of the Battyes to die on the field of honour, in the ranks of the Guides.

A touching proof of the affection and respect which his men had for him was most affectingly illustrated after the battle. There were, as in all armies, ambulance-bearers, whose duty it is to carry in litters the dead and wounded. For fear of desecration it was decided to send back the dead for burial to Jellalabad and beyond, and a litter was sent for Wigram Battye's mortal remains. But the rough warriors whose soldierly hearts he had won would allow of no such cortège. "Ambulance-bearers may be right and proper for anyone else," they said; "but our Sahib shall be carried by us soldiers, and by no one else." And so reverently they lifted the body of their dead comrade, and through the hot spring night carried it on the first stage towards the sweet spot in Mardan where the brothers Battye lie at rest.

But the silver lining to this dark cloud of loss was the prowess of the young subaltern and the squadron that had fallen to his charge. "Take 'em on, Walter, my boy," were his leader's last words; and right manfully did he obey them.

The plain over which they were advancing was somewhat undulating, covered with loose stones, and intersected here and there by more or less formidable nullahs. Across this not very promising cavalry country, Hamilton made good way, and was now close enough to the enemy to give the orders, "Gallop, Charge!" With the wild yell which so often, before and since, has struck chill to the heart of an enemy, the Guides dashed forward, the ground scouts checking back for the squadron to come up to them; but just as contact was imminent, a warning signal came from one of these that there was impassable ground in front. Here was a dilemma! Large masses of the enemy firing heavily close in front, an obstacle impassable for cavalry between, the guns uncomfortably threatened close by, and the infantry still some way off! Happily, however, it takes a good deal to stop a brave young Irishman with such men behind him. A second or two brought them to the obstacle, and sure enough it was no cold-blooded chance; a sheer nine foot drop into the dry bed of a stream, and opposite, with only a few yards interval, another sheer cliff, and on top of that an exulting and frenzied enemy! Without a moment's hesitation Hamilton jumped into the gulf, and after him, scrambling, sliding, jumping, anyhow and nohow, like a pack of hounds, streamed his fierce following. Like hounds, too, hot on the trail, they tarried not a moment there, but scattering up and down the nullah singly, or in clumps of two or three, found egress somehow. And then came death, and the Prophet's Paradise, to many a brave soul. From here and there, from front and right and left, by ones and twos, by threes and fours, charged home the gallant horsemen; and at their head, alone with his trumpeter, rode Hamilton. So rough and determined an onslaught would shake the nerves of even disciplined troops; but undrilled and undisciplined levies, however brave individually, cannot hope to stand the fiery blast of determined cavalry charging home. And so the great crowd broke, and for four long miles the pursuit continued, till man and horse alike were worn and tired, and arms became too stiff to strike or parry, and steeds yet willing staggered to a standstill.

In this brilliant charge the enemy lost four hundred men, while the squadron of the Guides lost twenty of all ranks and thirty-seven horses. To Walter Hamilton was awarded the Victoria Cross, and to six of his men the Order of Merit, for conspicuous gallantry where all were gallant.

* * * * *

Leaving many months of intervening history, we come to a notable feat of endurance, which threw a much needed reinforcement into Sherpur during the siege in December, 1879. The Guides were then strung along the lines of communication towards Jellalabad, but, on receipt of the serious news from Kabul, were at once concentrated forward towards the Jugdullak Pass, the scene of the massacre of our army in the old Afghan War. Hastening forward to the summit of the Lataband Pass, Jenkins got into communication by heliograph with Sir Frederick Roberts (as he then was), and learnt that reinforcements were urgently required. This was quite enough for the Commander of the Guides; he at once decided to make an effort to cross the thirty-six miles of mountainous country that intervened, and to fight his way single-handed through the great hordes of Afghans who were encircling Sherpur. Leaving the whole of their baggage, no mean sacrifice during an Afghan winter, and loading the mules with all the ammunition that could be carried, the Guides set cheerfully forth on their venture.

It is wonderful how often sheer boldness succeeds in warfare; here was a small body of troops marching forty miles *en l'air* through the enemy's fastnesses, and at the weary end unknown thousands blocking the way. With scarce a halt, horse and foot plodded on and on, till evening came and darkness fell, and still they marched along the dimly marked track. Near midnight the lights of Kabul and Sherpur became closely visible, and the crucial moment had arrived. But "by the kindness of God," as the ressaldar-major piously remarked, the night was very cold, Kabul lies six thousand feet above the sea, and a warm hut is better than an open field; and in fact, to make a long story short, the Afghans were keeping no watch on the road by which the Guides came, and thus the whole corps marched swiftly through the enemy's lines without firing a shot or losing a man. In Sherpur they were warmly welcomed by Sir Frederick Roberts and many old comrades, for, as at the siege of Delhi, the boldness, swiftness, and assuredness of their arrival added heartening and encouraging effect quite out of proportion to the numerical addition to the strength of the garrison.

During the next two days the Guides' infantry took part in the great assaults on the Takht-i-Shah, and the Asmai heights, with the 72nd and 92nd Highlanders; and in these Captain Fred Battye was dangerously wounded, and Captain A.G. Hammond[21] was awarded the Victoria Cross. In Sir Frederick Roberts's despatch the latter incident is thus recorded:

*Another officer who greatly distinguished himself on this occasion was Captain A.G. Hammond, Corps of Guides. He had been very forward during the storming of the As-*

---
21. Now Colonel Sir Arthur Hammond, V.C., D.S.O., K.C.B.

*mai heights, and now when the enemy were crowding up the western slopes, he remained with a few men on the ridge until the Afghans were within thirty yards of them. During the retirement one of the men of the Guides was shot; Captain Hammond stopped and assisted in carrying him away, though the enemy were at the time close by and firing heavily.*

No less than twelve men of the Guides also received the Order of Merit for conspicuous gallantry on this occasion.

As no result sufficient to counterbalance the serious losses incurred by making these repeated attacks on the enemy's position appeared to be obtained, Sir Frederick Roberts determined to alter his tactics, and to allow the enemy in their turn to hurl themselves against our defence. For a whole week, though in immensely superior numbers, the enemy could not steel their hearts to attack the fortified enclosure of Sherpur, where Roberts's small force lay entrenched. But on the evening of December 22nd certain information was received that a grand attack would take place at dawn, and that the signal for the advance would be a beacon which would be kindled on the Asmai heights, just above the village of Deh-i-Afghan.

Strict watch was kept that night in the British lines, and after the keen anxiety of the long vigil a feeling almost of relief passed through the staunch defenders when, about half-an-hour before daylight, the beacon shone forth that waved to the attack the followers of the Prophet, to wipe the hated infidel from the face of God's earth.

In the intense stillness of the frosty winter's night the swift shuffling tramp of thousands of sandalled feet could be heard coming across the open. The attack was evidently aimed at the eastern face of Sherpur, rightly considered the weakest point structurally, but stoutly and steadfastly held by the Guides. Where such immensely superior numbers are concerned it is not safe to allow them to get too close, or by sheer weight they may beat down a thin line of rifle-fire. The Guides consequently opened a heavy fire into the darkness in the direction of the advancing masses, thereby making known to all and sundry that the surprise, as a surprise, had failed. This with undisciplined troops was alone enough to disconcert the whole operation; the enemy, instead of advancing, halted, and, taking refuge in the villages, awaited the break of day.

So soon as it was light they opened a heavy but badly aimed fire on the Guides, but showed no disposition to assault. At last, after some delay and evidently under the urgent haranguing of their priests and leaders, a mass of warriors some five thousand strong was collected under the shelter of the villages to make another effort. But so steady and accurate was the fire of the Guides, that even these brave fanatics feared to face the open, and the attack melted away. Sir Frederick Roberts, with the eye of the born general seizing the right moment, launched his cavalry and artillery in counterstroke and pursuit, till when the sun set that night fifty thousand of the chivalry of the Afghan nation had been swept from sight and hearing, and nothing but a vast solitude remained where teeming thousands stood lately.

Thus collect, and thus disappear, the great yeomen armies of Afghanistan. To-day they are not; to-morrow they are assembling in their thousands from the four quarters of the compass; a few days, and they have melted away like snow. The explanation is simple enough. The fiery crescent goes forth, summoning the faithful, every man with his arms and ammunition and carrying in his goatskin bag food enough to last him for a week. Commissariat or Ordnance Departments there are none; thus as each soldier finishes his food or his ammunition, or both, he hies him home again for a fresh supply; perhaps he returns, and perhaps he has had enough fighting for the present, and does not. And so is it with all the fifty thousand.

The Guides did not see any more serious fighting till April, when, together with a wing of the 92nd Highlanders under Major White,[22] and two guns of F.-A. Battery, Royal Horse Artillery, they fought a gallant little action with about five thousand of the enemy at Charasiab near Kabul. Jenkins, who was in command, heard shortly after midnight that about two thousand of the enemy were bivouacked within five miles of the camp, but that they had no immediate intention of attacking. An old soldier like the Commander of the Guides, however, takes nothing for granted, and orders were at once issued for the Guides' infantry to stand to their arms an hour before daylight, while the Guides' cavalry sent out patrols to feel for the enemy at crack of dawn. And well was it that these timely precautions were taken, for as day broke the enemy's masses were seen advancing to the attack. To give elbow-room, and also as a preparation for all eventualities, Jenkins struck his camp, and ordered the baggage to be stacked behind a convenient mound; then sending back word of how matters stood to Sir Frederick Roberts, he with his little force prepared to face the onslaught.

Seizing such knolls and points of vantage as existed, his battle-line took the form of a semicircle, with one company of the 92nd Highlanders and two companies of the Guides in reserve. The enemy, now increased to three thousand warriors, steadily advanced, and with great bravery planted their standards in some places within one hundred yards of the British line; but that last one hundred yards they could not, by all the eloquence of their leaders or the promises of Paradise from their

---

22. Afterwards Field-Marshal Sir George White, V.C., G.C.B., &c., &c.

priests, be induced to cross. Nor was it only the Afghans who felt the tightening strain; it was an anxious moment for the British, too, for given one slight slip, one weak-hearted corner, and the whole thin line might have been swept away by the onslaught of those fierce masses.

It was then that Jenkins used a curious and expensive, but, as it proved, effective expedient. He ordered the Guides' cavalry to mount, and, exposed at close range to the enemy's fire, to patrol quietly from one end of the line to the other, as a sort of moving reserve; a demonstration, in fact, that even if the enemy managed to break through the thin line of the infantry at any point, it would only be to fall on the dreaded swords of the cavalry. The behaviour of the men during this trying ordeal was above all praise; and indeed it requires high qualities of nerve and courage to walk one's horse up and down for a couple of hours under a hail of bullets, without being able to return the compliment in any way.

The enemy's numbers had increased to five thousand, and still Jenkins's little force held on with dogged courage, and though it could not make an inch of way, it refused to concede one. It was now past one o'clock, and the strain lay heavy on our men after seven hours of this bull-dog business; when the twinkle of the cheerful heliograph from Kabul gave fresh heart to all, and almost immediately afterwards the advance skirmishers of General Macpherson's column came into view, and the situation was saved. Then, borne on the flood of the reinforcements, Highlanders and Guides sprang to their feet and dashed at the now flying enemy. The cavalry and artillery, too, at last relieved of their long and dangerous vigil, dashed off in pursuit, and for four long miles they fell with relentless fury on the scattered and demoralised foe.

This was the last fight which the Guides had in the

Afghan War. When Roberts and his gallant ten thousand marched to Kandahar, they were sent back to their hard-earned rest, after two years of incessant warfare, with a casualty roll of two hundred and forty-eight of all ranks and one hundred and forty-two horses; and with five hundred recruits to redress the balance.

## Chapter 10
# War Stories

Several months before the Afghan War began the Guides were placed on guard at the mouth of the Khyber Pass, and there occurred an incident which illustrates the extremely delicate problem accompanying the employment of Indian troops in certain situations. In the ranks of the Guides are men belonging to a great number of tribes and nationalities, many of them enlisted from amongst peoples whose territories lie outside the British borders. It may so happen therefore, and indeed does happen, that in the kaleidoscope of events a man who has taken service and sworn to fight the battles of the King finds himself called upon to attack his own village, and possibly to raise his rifle against his own kith and kin. Such a situation naturally requires very careful handling. It is of course absolutely necessary to maintain the great principle, that a soldier is bound hand and foot and in all honour to the service of his Sovereign, and that no family or private ties must stand between him and any duty that service may call on him to perform. On the other hand, without relinquishing this principle, it is often possible, by a little tactful and unostentatious redistribution of troops, to avoid placing a soldier in so unenviable a position as taking part in an attack on his own home. Sometimes, however, this is impossible, as in the story here related.

The Guides were daily expecting orders to advance into the Khyber Pass at the head of an army, and would thus at the very outset be fighting against some of the men's own relations and friends. Amongst these men was a young

Afridi soldier, who was sore puzzled what to do. His own village lay right in the path of the army, and only a few miles distant; his relations and friends came daily to visit him, urging him to take his discharge and return to his own people before the war began. Was anyone ever in a more awkward position?

On the very eve of the advance he made his decision to stand by the colours, and gave a final refusal to his relations. Yet even then opportunity, combined with the ties of kinship, was too much for him. It was his turn for sentry-go that night, all double sentries, and, as is the custom, no two men of the same class together. With our young Afridi on his beat there happened to be a Gurkha, and that Gurkha did a thing which not only hurled his comrade to perdition, but brought himself to a court-martial. His tent was close by and he said to the young Afridi: "Hold my rifle a minute, while I fetch something from my tent." In one second the whole of that young Afridi's good resolutions failed him; the struggle of weeks had been in vain. Two rifles in his hand, not a soul near, the black night in front, and beyond--his own village, and friends, and a warm welcome! He stalked off into the darkness and was lost for ever. Then came the sequel.

The British officers were at dinner in their mess tent, when the havildar of the guard came running up to make his report, and brought as witness the erring Gurkha. The Colonel of the Corps at this time was Colonel F. H. Jenkins, a man who had learnt much from Lumsden, and had caught in many ways the genius for dealing with wild warriors. "How many men of that man's tribe are there in the regiment?" sternly demanded Jenkins. After reference to the company, it was found that there were seventeen of them all told. "Parade them all here," said the Colonel; and they were duly summoned, and paraded in line. "Now take off every scrap of uniform or equipment that belongs to the

Types of men in the Guides' Infantry

Sirkar." Each man did as he was bid, and placed the little pile in front of him, on the ground. "You can now go, and don't let me see your faces again till you bring back those two rifles."

The Colonel perhaps hoped that they might overtake the fugitive, overpower and secure him before he had gone far; but if so he was disappointed, for as day followed day, and week succeeded week, no news came of pursued or pursuers. The matter had been forgotten; the vacancies had long since been filled; indeed, two whole years had passed, when one day there walked into Mardan Cantonment a ragged, rough-bearded, hard-bitten gang of seventeen men, carrying two rifles. It was the lost legion!

Of those two years' toil and struggle, wounds received and given, a stark unburied corpse here and there on the mountain-side, days in ambush and bitter nights of silent anxious watch, they spoke but little. But their faces beamed with honest pride as their spokesmen simply said: "The Sahib told us never to show our faces again until we found the rifles, and here they are. Now, by your Honour's kindness, we will again enlist and serve the Queen."

\* \* \* \* \*

On another occasion, during the Afghan War, it was a matter of considerable importance to ascertain the temper of an important tribe, whose position and territory threatened the left flank of the lines of communication not far short of Jellalabad. For this difficult and dangerous duty Duffadar Faiz Talab of the Guides offered his services, well knowing the great risks he was likely to incur, though, as the event proved, he materially underrated them.

Dressed as an ordinary Pathan, with great flowing white garments, a slatey blue puggery, and with a dagger or two stuck in his cummerband, he sallied forth one dark night, and laid up not far from camp. This precaution was taken so that not one of the hundreds of pairs of sharp eyes in our own camp should see him depart.

Next day he strolled on leisurely, and in the course of the afternoon arrived at the chief village of the tribe in question. In every Afghan village there is a rest-house, or serai, for strangers, and thither as a rule towards evening the village gossips also find their way; the hospitable hookah is passed from mouth to mouth, and in grave Oriental fashion they set about picking each other's gossip-pockets. "And you, brave stranger, who are you?" asked a grey-bearded, sharp-eyed old man of Duffadar Faiz Talab.

"I?" he answered readily; "why, I have just left those dogs of Feringhis (may God burn them in hell!), where I took service for a short time, so as to learn their ways, and their tricks of fighting."

"Shahbash (bravo)!" exclaimed the company; "and what are you going to do now?"

"What am I going to do now? Why, fight the accursed infidels, of course!" replied the duffadar.

"That is indeed fortunate," said the headman of the village, "for our spies tell us that the Feringhis intend attacking us. We shall now be able to make you the general of our forces, and since you have been so wise as to learn the cunning strategy of the infidels we shall of a surety kill them all, and send their souls to hell."

"Oh yes, certainly, if I am here," hastily murmured Faiz Talab, adding as he regained his composure and the Oriental art of fluently telling the thing that is not true, "but unfortunately I have urgent business over the Khost, and cannot delay. To-morrow at crack of dawn I must be on my way."

"Our kismet is indeed bad, but let the will of God be done!" was the pious rejoinder of the most villainous-looking of the surrounding cut-throats.

Night having now fallen, and the lighting arrangements of an Afghan village being limited to a wood fire, travellers and villagers began one by one to roll themselves up in their wadded quilts, and each man, hugging his sword, dropped off to sleep.

Just before dawn Faiz Talab was awakened by someone rudely shaking him. "Get up, oh indolent one, the English are upon us, and we look to you to help us to defeat them. Here, take this rifle and these twenty rounds of ammunition, and come and show us how best we may arrange our battle line."

Up jumped the duffadar, and hastily shook together his sleeping wits. Here was a pretty dilemma! Evidently something had occurred to precipitate action on the part of the British, and it had been found inexpedient, or perhaps impossible, to wait for the receipt of his report. Meanwhile the duffadar was in the exceedingly uncomfortable position of him who finds himself between the devil and the deep sea. As the chosen leader, thus miraculously fallen from heaven on the eve of battle, he had become so important a figure that it was impossible for him to take up a modest position in the rear; indeed, a bullet through the head would have been the immediate rejoinder to any such suggestion on his part. Forced thus by circumstance into the forefront of the battle, he turned his back to the devil and stood forth to face the deep sea, and the great waves of British soldiers which surged across it to the attack.

"The first thing to do," he shouted authoritatively, "is to take good cover, so that the bullets and cannon-balls of the English cannot hit us; and then, when they have expended their ammunition, we will shout Allah! and charge them with the sword."

"Well spoken!" was the cry, and the order passed up and down the line.

Be assured that duffadar Faiz Talab did not fail to appropriate the thickest and strongest wall in support of his tactical scheme.

"The next thing to do," yelled the unwilling general, "is to fire as rapidly as possible, so as to frighten the English thoroughly, before we sally forth and kill them." And suiting action to words Faiz Talab fired off his twenty rounds with great rapidity in the safest possible direction, and prayed God that he had not hit one of his own comrades. At the same time he added a perhaps equally potent supplication, to the effect that his comrades might not be so careless or inconsiderate in their turn as to shoot him.

Having no more ammunition, Faiz Talab hugged his wall closer than a limpet, and noticed with growing satisfaction that ammunition was running out all along the line. On the other hand, as an inquisitive neighbour, with two bullets in his puggery, pointed out, the English were advancing very quickly, apparently with plenty of ammunition, and were just at that moment fixing bayonets.

"Fixing bayonets!" exclaimed one and all; "then it is indeed necessary that we should depart, so that, by the grace of God, we may be ready to fight with renewed vigour on another day."

"That is well spoken, brethren," said Faiz Talab, and added with considerable pathos, "but as for me, I shall remain and die at my post."

"Oh, say not so!" remarked one or two with polite, but not very insistent interest.

"Nothing will persuade me to move," stubbornly reiterated the duffadar, devoutly praying that no one else would insist on sharing his bed of glory.

The English soldiers could now be heard talking plainly, and one, speaking louder than the rest, said, "Cease firing, fix bayonets, charge!" A loud hurrah! sounded, and then Faiz Talab found himself alone on his side of the wall. That was all very well, but it was not of much avail to have escaped so far, to end his days with eighteen inches of a British bayonet through his best embroidered waistcoat. If it had been any Indian regiment, or, better still, his own regiment, the Guides, he could at once have secured safety by declaring who he was. But with British soldiers, none of whom would probably understand a word he said, and all heated with the excitement of battle, he might get the bayonet first and enquiry afterwards. However, something had to be done; so up he jumped and, holding up his hands, yelled, "Stop! stop! I am a friend of the British."

"'Ullo, 'ere's another bloomin' ghazi! 'ave at 'im, Bill!" was the brisk rejoinder, in the familiar tongue of a British soldier of the 17th Foot.

And "'ave at 'im" they most assuredly would, had not a British officer arrived in the very nick of time. "He says he is a friend of the British," the officer shouted; "give him quarter till we find out whether he speaks the truth or not."

So reluctantly they made Faiz Talab a prisoner, temporarily postponing the pleasure of sending him to join his numerous friends in the ghazis' Paradise.

But Faiz Talab said to the officer: "May I see you alone? I have something important to tell you."

"Yes, certainly," said the officer; "but mind, one of my men covers you all the time."

And when they drew apart, Faiz Talab took off his shoe; under the lining was a little piece of paper, which he handed to the officer, and on it was written in English: The bearer of this is Duffadar Faiz Talab of the Guides: please give him every assistance.--F.H. Jenkins, Lt.-Col.

# Chapter 11
# Adventures of Shah Sowar & Abdul Mujid

Many strange adventures have befallen individual men of the Guides, and many a hairbreadth escape have they had. It was only a few years ago that the following adventures occurred.

An order reached regimental headquarters to detail a cavalry soldier who could speak Persian, and one stout of heart and limb, to accompany a British officer on a mission of considerable danger and uncertainty. He was to call at a certain house, on a certain day, in Karachi, and to ask for the name of Smith. Shah Sowar was the trooper selected, and when he arrived at the place of tryst he was ushered into the presence of Smith. Smith, however, was not Smith at all, but somebody quite different; not that it mattered much, for Smith was only his Karachi name.

Next day, on board ship, he became the Sheikh Abdul Qadir, on his way to Mecca or where not; and from that moment commenced the troubles of the redoubtable Shah Sowar. To anyone who has the least knowledge of Asia the extraordinary difficulty which any European must experience in disguising himself as a man of an Eastern race will be apparent. By dint of living for years as Asiatics, exceptional linguists like Vambery and Burton have undoubtedly been able to pass unchallenged, but anyone possessing qualities short of theirs must inevitably be discovered a dozen times a day. The way we eat and drink, the way we walk and sit, the way we wear

Types of men in the Guides' Cavalry, both in uniform and mufti

our clothes and boots, the way we wash,--every little thing is absolutely different from the methods and manners of the East.

These things Shah Sowar pointed out with much politeness, and great persistency, to Sheikh Abdul Qadir, late Smith. "Be it spoken with the greatest respect, but there would be less liability to the unmannerly curiosity of strangers if the Cherisher of the Poor wore his own clothes. Beautifully as your Highness speaks Persian and Hindustani [his Highness really spoke both indifferently] it would be difficult for one of such commanding presence to pass himself for any but an Englishman. English officers are a race of princes; how then can they disguise themselves as inferior folk?"

"Don't fret," replied Smith, alias Sheikh Abdul Qadir; "I am going to remain a prince all right; for I propose passing myself off as a near relation of the Amir, a refugee from Kabul."

"As your Honour wishes," was the resigned reply; but Shah Sowar saw big rollers ahead.

Arrived on the coasts of Persia (it matters not where), Sheikh Abdul Qadir, Shah Sowar, and a cook-boy landed as refugees from Kabul, on their way to place their swords and services at the disposal of the Shah of Persia.

In these days an officer with a Government permit might probably travel, with a moderate escort, in perfect safety throughout Persia; but at that time a Government permit, and a small escort, would merely have served to draw the unwelcome attention of the hordes of robbers who infested the country. For good and sufficient reasons our friend Smith was required to pass through a certain tract of very unsettled country on his journey, ways and means being left to his own ingenuity.

As Shah Sowar had foretold, the first serious pitfall was the question of language. When persons of some rank are travelling it is customary for the headman, or chief, to come and pay his respects to them, when they are encamped near his village or domain. It was after one such visit that the chief, as he came out, called Shah Sowar to him and said: "Who did you say that your master is?"

"Commander of the Faithful, his name is Sheikh Abdul Qadir, a relative of the Amir of Kabul and a refugee," glibly replied Shah Sowar, but inwardly considerably perturbed.

"Well, with all respect," replied the chief, "I never heard anyone talk such bad Persian; he talks just like an Englishman"; and with that he departed.

Shah Sowar at once grasped what a narrow escape they had had, for an Englishman found in that region in disguise was a dead man. So soon therefore as it was dark he persuaded his master to saddle and move on a few miles, lest further reflection might shed a light on the dim suspicions of the chief. One bargain Shah Sowar made during that night march, and that was that Sheikh Abdul Qadir was henceforth to remain speechless, and leave the rest to his own ingenuity and knowledge of his countrymen.

A few days afterwards an occasion offered for testing the new arrangement. Arrived at a somewhat important town, a servant of the local chief came to make enquiries about the new arrivals, in order that the etiquette of visiting might be observed, this etiquette ruling that the inferior should pay the first visit. Here Shah Sowar at once took a high hand, insisting that his master, from his princely connections, held the higher rank and must be visited first. "But," he added in a confidential whisper, "my master is an extraordinary man; some days he is as lively as a bulbul and laughs and talks with everyone; on others he sits silent and morose and will not utter a word. Be it spoken in confidence, but I think he must be mad. At any rate, prepare your master. If to-day happen to be one of his bad days, then that is kismet and your master must excuse." Having thus prepared one side, he placed a bed across the end of the tent and asked Sheikh Abdul Qadir, late Smith, to sit cross-legged on it, to glare fixedly and furiously into vacancy, and to grunt at intervals, but on no account to utter a syllable.

In due course the chief and his retinue arrived, and were met with great politeness and many salaams by Shah Sowar; but that worthy managed to whisper in the chief's ear the sad intelligence that this was one of his master's bad days, and that the Evil Spirit was upon him. "Nevertheless be pleased to enter," he added aloud; "His Highness will be glad to see you."

The exceedingly restricted area of the tent prevented a large assembly, but the chief, his brother, and Shah Sowar managed to squeeze in and squat down. After exchanging salutations the chief gravely stroked his beard, and gave vent to a few polite expressions of welcome. To these Sheikh Abdul Qadir vouchsafed no reply beyond a grunt. The chief glanced at Shah Sowar, and that excellent comedian, assuming the ashamed look of one disgraced by his master's rudeness, at once made a long-winded and complimentary reply in the most fluent and high-flown Persian. Then, before the effect should be lost, he ordered in tea, and commenced an animated conversation with the two strangers, all parties absolutely ignoring, out of politeness, Sheikh Abdul Qadir and his Evil Spirit. Thus anxiously skating over the thin ice, Shah Sowar at last, with a feeling of infinite relief, bowed out the visitors, charmed with his excellent manners and quite unsuspecting that they had sat for half-an-hour within two feet of a British officer. When the time for the return visit came, Shah Sowar went alone to make the readily accepted excuse that his master was not in a fit state that day to fulfil social obligations.

Thus the ready wit and resource of Shah Sowar piloted the party through many dangerous waters, till one day they chanced across a nomad tribe under a venerable white-bearded chief, who could count a thousand spears at his beck and call. The usual visits of ceremony had been paid and tided over somehow, and the travellers were resting during the heat of the afternoon, when a confidential servant of the White Beard came to Shah Sowar and said that his master had sent for him. A peremptory call like this boded no good, but by way of getting a further puff to show which way the wind blew, Shah Sowar assumed a haughty air. "Peace be unto you," he said; "there is no hurry. I will come when I am sufficiently rested, and have received permission from my own master." "Be advised by me, who wish you no harm, to come at once, as the matter is of importance," replied the messenger. "Oh, very well," grumbled Shah Sowar, feeling that trouble was in the air; "I will come."

When he arrived at the camp of the White Beard he was immediately ushered into his tent, and there found the old warrior seated cross-legged on a rich carpet, and gravely stroking his beard. "Look here, Shah Sowar," said he with soldierly directness, "it is no good lying to me. That is a sahib you have with you. I have been to Bushire, and I know an Englishman when I see him."

Shah Sowar was prepared for this, but, by way of gaining time, he answered: "Your Excellency's cleverness is extraordinary; to lie to your Highness would be the work only of a fool. Perchance my master may be a sahib, but there are many nations of sahibs, and why should this one be English?" "Peace, prattler!" sternly replied the old autocrat; "there is only one nation of real sahibs, and they are English."

Shah Sowar, driven into a corner, stroked his beard for some time under the rebuke, and then said: "I perceive there is no good trying to deceive so great a diviner as you. I will speak the truth. My master is an English officer travelling on business. What then?"

"What then?" slowly replied the White Beard. "Why, I have sworn on the Koran, and before all my tribe, to kill every Englishman I come across. I fear no nation on earth but the English, and lest they swallow me up, I have sworn to swallow them, one by one, whenever I meet them."

"If your Honour has thus sworn there is nothing else to be said," answered Shah Sowar. "But I have one petition to make, and that is to give us till the morning before we die."

"Your petition is granted; but why say 'we'? I shall not kill you, for you are a Mahomedan, and a Persian, and shall join my horsemen," said the White Beard.

"When the Sahib dies, I die also," was the brave reply. And with that Shah Sowar hurried back to tell the bad news to his master. Arrived at their little camp, his worst forebodings were confirmed, for a strong detachment of the White Beard's men guarded it on every side.

All that afternoon the prisoners racked their brains to find a way of escape, and hope seemed to die with the setting sun. Then Shah Sowar arose and said, "I will have one more try to see what can be done"; and gaining permission, he went over again to the chief's camp, and asked for another audience. The old man was at his prayers, and Shah Sowar devoutly and humbly joined in. When they had finished he asked for a private audience, as he had something of importance to say.

"Well, what is it?" said the White Beard when they were alone.

"It is this," gravely replied the Guides' trooper, "and be pleased to listen attentively. When you bade me speak the truth this afternoon, I spoke fearlessly and at once. I acknowledged that my Sahib is an English officer. Hear now also the truth, and on the Koran I am prepared to swear it. This English officer whom you propose to kill is the bearer of an important letter to the Shah of Persia, and

I swear to you by Allah and all his prophets that, should harm befall him, for every hair of his head the Shah will kill one of your horsemen. Make calculation, oh venerable one; has not the Sahib more than a thousand hairs on his head? I have spoken. Now do your worst, but blame not me afterwards."

"This is very unfortunate," said the much perturbed chieftain. "Have I not sworn before all my people? How then can I now spare this Englishman? My kismet is indeed bad; I can see no road of escape."

"That I can show you," said Shah Sowar, "and for that am I come again."

"Say on, I am listening."

"You have sworn before your people that you will kill the Englishman at dawn; but there is no reason why the Englishman should not escape during the night. To save your face I will heavily bribe one of the sentries, and we will escape on foot leaving everything behind. Thus you will get all our horses, and mules, and tents, and all that we have. And in the morning you can say 'It was the will of God,' and march away in the opposite direction."

"You have spoken well," said the chief after deep thought. "I will do as you wish; it is the will of God." Then he added aloud, and with anger so that all might hear: "I have spoken; at dawn the accursed Englishman shall die, and I will shoot him with mine own hand. Praise be to Allah, and Mahomed the prophet of Allah."

So Shah Sowar went back to his Sahib and explained the plan of escape. And as soon as all was still the three slipped noiselessly out of the camp, past the bribed sentry, and, setting their faces to the south, toiled on, hiding at intervals, till they had placed well-nigh forty miles between themselves and the camp of the White Bearded Chief.

Then his heart broke through the stiff reserve of the Englishman, and he embraced his gallant comrade, and said: "You and I are no longer master and servant, sahib and trooper; you have saved my life and henceforth we are brothers. What can I do for you to show my gratitude?"

"Nothing, Sahib, except to tell my Colonel that I have done good service and upheld the name of the Guides." And the only other thing that Shah Sowar would accept was a watch to replace that which he had lost in the flight; and on it is inscribed, To my faithful friend Shah Sowar in memory of--(and here follows the date of their flight).

* * * * *

Amongst the explorers who have gone forth from the Guides, taking their lives in their hands and barely escaping, was one Abdul Mujid. This fine specimen of the trained adventurer was working through a hitherto unmapped and little known country, when one evening he came to a small village, and made his way as usual to the travellers' serai. There also, as is not unusual, he found assembled, besides wayfarers like himself, the headman of the village and two or three other residents, smoking and chatting. They made room for Abdul Mujid, and with the outwardly polite insistence of the Oriental asked his business, whence he came, and whither he was going.

While our good friend the Guide was spinning such romances as seemed good unto him, to account for his presence in this secluded valley, a small boy came and squatted down at his feet, to lose not a word of the story. And sitting there, like a boy, or a magpie, he picked up one of the shoes which Abdul Mujid had slipped off as he took his seat and began to examine it curiously. This perfectly childish act by chance caught the wandering glance of the headman, and as he looked at the shoes, and then up at the fine strapping fellow who owned them, a sudden thought occurred to him. "Those are very like soldiers' shoes," he said in a hard, suspicious voice; "I have seen them wearing the like in Peshawur."

Abdul Mujid was considerably taken aback, for it had never occurred to him that in these wild parts he might chance across anyone who had travelled far enough to know the difference between a soldier's and any other shoe. However, his ready wit came to his service, and with scarce a pause he replied quietly: "Yes, I bought them in one of the border villages from a sepoy on leave," and then turned the conversation on to less dangerous ground. But he saw he was suspected, and any moment might find him seized and searched. It was too late to move on to another village; indeed to attempt to do so would only serve to confirm suspicion, and the moment he had passed the sacred portals of hospitality he would have been instantly followed and cut down.

Shoes in themselves are not enough to hang a man, but a prismatic compass assuredly is. In a Pathan country murder, rapine, and cattle-lifting are comparatively venial offences, little more indeed than instances of lightheartedness; but to draw a map of the country is worse than the seven deadly sins rolled into one, and short will be the shrift of him who is caught in the act. It therefore seemed to Abdul Mujid only a wise precaution to get rid of his prismatic compass as speedily as possible.

With this end in view he walked over to the well, as if to get a drink of water, and, as skilfully as he could, dropped the compass down the well. But fate was against him that day; sharp ears heard the hollow splash, and sharp voices immediately demanded what he had thrown down the well.

"Only a stone off the coping," replied Abdul Mujid.

"You lie!" yelled the headman. "You are a spy of the accursed British Government, and out of your own mouth will I condemn you. Here, Yusuf, get a stout rope and let the boy down the well; there isn't more than half a yard of water in it, and we will soon see whether the stranger lies or not."

Here was a nice predicament! But Abdul Mujid faced the peril like a man, and held to the faint hope that no one would recognise the instrument even if they found it. It was a false hope. In a few minutes up came the boy, gleefully flourishing the damning evidence, and there was not one who doubted what it was. Probably in the circumstances, whatever the article it would have had the same effect, for the case was already prejudiced.

"Now then, thou son of a burnt father, what sayest thou?" screamed the headman. "Thou art a spy as I said, and shalt surely die. Hein! what sayest thou?"

"You speak truth, father," replied the sepoy. "I am making a map for the British Government; but this is only a little portion of it, and if you object I will leave out this part altogether, and then there can be no cause of offence."

"Go to," sneered the headman, "I shall take a much more effective way of closing the matter by killing you at once. Here, Yusuf, bring my gun, and you, young men, see that this misbegotten Kafir does not escape."

So Yusuf went off for the gun, and Abdul Mujid turned his face towards Mecca, and said the evening prayer. Then hope came to him from above and he said to the headman: "Be not hasty; I am a follower of the Prophet as also are ye. Give me till the morning that I may make my peace with Allah."

"It is well said," interposed a bystander; "he is alone and has no chance of escape. Let us therefore not kill him like a dog or an infidel; but let him make his peace with Allah, and then in the morning he shall die."

And so it was settled, and Abdul Mujid was bound hand and foot, and laid upon a charpoy[23]; and beside him, with a drawn sword at his side, lay down the man who was to guard him, the two on the same bed.

---

23. Charpoy, the common bed of the country.

All night long Abdul Mujid lay racking his brains for a means of escape, and found none; and then just before dawn came Allah to his help. Nudging his bedfellow hard, the sepoy said: "Awake, sluggard, I wish to go and pray."

"Well, go and pray," grumbled the guard.

"Go and pray!" replied Abdul Mujid; "how can I go and pray with my arms and feet tied? Can I make the salutations and genuflections ordered in the Koran while thus strapped up?"

"No, I suppose you can't," answered the guard. "But you also don't suppose I am going to leave my warm quilt on this bitterly cold morning to guard you while you pray?"

"That is not the least necessary," said Abdul Mujid; "if you will free one hand I will spread my own carpet by the bed, and you can thus guard me without getting up, for my legs are tied, and therefore I cannot escape. Assuredly Allah hath spread the cloak of stupidity and sloth over this fellow," he said to himself, as his janitor rolled over, and lazily muttering "Oh very well, anything for a little peace," to the sepoy's intense delight fumblingly untied one of his hands.

What followed was like a streak of lightning from heaven. In one flash Abdul Mujid had seized the naked sword, and the slothful sentry, before he could draw another breath, lay dead to all below; in another flash he had severed his bonds, and was making the best of his way across the fields. Nor did he halt, night or day, till weary and exhausted he fell down and slept by the first milestone that proclaimed that he was again in British territory.

Nearly a year afterwards a motley band of ruffians might have been seen walking up the main road at Mardan towards the Court-House. It was a deputation from a far-away country come to discuss matters with the political officer. At their head on a sorry steed rode the chief person: at the roadside by the post-office, idly watching the party file past, was a man of the Guides; and when the eyes of those two, the Guide and the man on the pony, met, they both remembered the village well, and one recollected how nearly it was his last night on earth.

"May you never grow weary," said the Guide in the polite formula of the road.

"May your riches ever increase," came the stock reply.

"And how about that man on the charpoy?" bawled Abdul Mujid.

"Oh, he's all right, having by the mercy of God a thick skull," came the reply.

"Shahbash! come and feast with me when your business is finished. I will make preparations at the cook-shop at the head of the bazaar."

And so ended in peace and jollification an adventure which at one time looked much more like cold-blooded murder and a string of vendettas.

# Chapter 12
# The Relief of Chitral

The anxiety of great events in South Africa has somewhat dimmed the recollection of our smaller troubles in previous years; but perhaps there are some who can recall the feeling of tense suspense that enthralled the nation during the spring of 1895.

Two hundred miles from our borders in an inaccessible, and hitherto almost unheard of, valley lay besieged a little force of Indian soldiers, under the command of a sprinkling of British officers. Between the beleaguered garrison and the nearest support lay great chains of the highest mountains in the world, still covered thick in snow, rivers deep and strong and of incredible treachery, roads that were mere goat-tracks carried along the face of precipices, or following a shingly bed between stupendous walls of rock, many made doubly perilous by craftily prepared stone-shoots. To add to the difficulties of the task climatic variations of extraordinary diversity had to be overcome, for troops might one day be freezing on a pass twenty thousand feet above the sea, and on another sweltering under the tropical heat of the valley below; days passed under the scorching rays of an Eastern sun might be succeeded by nights without shelter under storms of cold and pitiless rain. Finally one of the two relief columns had to pass through two hundred miles of unmapped and unexplored country, inhabited by armed fanatical tribes fiercely opposed to the passage of the troops while the other, weak in numbers, and marching *en l'air* hundreds of miles from any support, was a veritable forlorn hope.

It speaks highly for the mobilisation arrangements of the Indian Army that within eleven days a corps of all arms, twenty-five thousand strong, had derailed at a little roadside station, and under Sir Robert Low had marched forty-two miles to the frontier, fought a decisive action, and forced the first barrier of mountains on its road to Chitral. Unhappily it does not lie within the region of this story to relate how the gallant forlorn hope under Colonel Kelly, overcoming stupendous difficulties, made its way to the succour of the sore beset garrison, but history has already done justice to that gallant achievement. Here, in a regimental narrative we are naturally restricted to the column to which the Guides belonged.

On the opening day of the campaign it fell to the Guides' infantry to turn the right flank of the enemy, having, supported by the 4th Sikhs, captured after five hours' hard fighting a commanding mountain, to this day called the Guides' Hill, which completely dominated and turned the Malakand position. It was next day, however, that a weak squadron of the Guides' cavalry had the opportunity of performing a notable service. After the passage of the Malakand the road runs down between gently sloping spurs into the Swat Valley. At the end of one of these spurs was a rocky outcrop, which would now be called a kopje, and holding this was a regiment of Dogras, while in support, under cover, lay the best part of a brigade of infantry. Just under the tail end of the kopje stood dismounted a squadron, fifty strong, of the Guides, under Captain Adams and Lieutenant Baldwin. The neighbouring hills were covered with dense masses of the enemy, firing heavily, and severely pressing the Dogras. Evening was drawing on and the day too far advanced for the British force to commit itself to any very forward or extended operations.

At this moment a temporary non-combatant, the well-known Roddy Owen, then acting as a newspaper correspondent, in the course of doing a little scouting on his own account discovered a large force of the enemy, estimated at two thousand men, committed to the open with the evident intention of enveloping the left flank of the Dogras. This news he at once communicated to Captain Adams, and that officer rode back a short distance to take the General's orders. Just as he was returning, Lieutenant Baldwin, seeing that the moment to strike had arrived, boldly took the initiative and set off on his gallant venture. The effect was little short of magical, and established irrevocably the moral of cavalry and the arme blanche for the rest of the campaign. The moment the little squadron of the Guides appeared round the corner, yelling the well-known war-whoop of the Indian soldier, the whole of the forward movement of the enemy's masses ceased. There was a moment of hesitation, another of delay, and then the whole body broke and fled, fiercely pursued by the cavalry. The execution done was considerable, but greater still was the moral effect. From that day forth a mounted man was a power in the land.

The Relief Force now pushed across the Swat River, and over the Saram range of mountains, and came in due course to the formidable Panjkora River, formidable not so much from its size, or breadth, but from its great rapidity and uncertainty. In a single night, fed by melting snow from the higher levels, it would rise from twelve to fourteen feet. And this is exactly what happened at a critical moment, when it fell to the honour of the Guides to avert a serious disaster.

Before the Relief Force could cross it was necessary to bridge the river, and this was done at a narrow part. Directly it was completed the Guides were ordered across to hold the bridge-head, and thus cover the passage of the main body next morning. That the defence might not be a passive one only, Lieutenant-Colonel Fred Battye,

Non-commissioned Officer and Trooper of the Guides' Cavalry

who was commanding, was ordered at dawn to push out, destroy all the neighbouring villages, and turn the enemy out of all positions from which they had been operating during the construction of the bridge, and from which they could harass the passage of the force. During the night a freshet came down, the river rose fourteen feet, and the newly finished bridge was swept away. The Guides were thus isolated on the far bank, but getting no orders to the contrary, and very possibly thinking that to remain inactive was to invite unwelcome attention to their condition, Colonel Battye decided to adhere to the original programme. Therefore leaving two companies at the site of the broken bridge, he at six in the morning moved out to drive back the enemy's outposts, and destroy such villages as were troublesome.

Up to nine o'clock there was no opposition to speak of. Colonel Battye then formed the five companies of the Guides, which constituted his force, into three small columns, and was proceeding to carry out more extended operations, when, from the high ground now occupied, dense masses of the enemy, afterwards officially estimated at from seven to ten thousand, were seen rapidly approaching his right flank. It had evidently become known to the enemy that the bridge was broken, and that the Guides were cut off by an impassable river from all support. The matter was immediately reported by heliograph to Sir Robert Low, and orders as promptly sent for the Guides to retire on the bridge-head.

It is on an occasion like this that the true fighting value of a regiment shows itself. Great as is the glory of those who, surrounded by comrades, are borne on the tide of great events to victory, still greener are the laurels that adorn the standards of those who, amidst great tribulation and fighting against overwhelming odds, keep untarnished their ancient fame.

Before the anxious eyes of an army, so near yet so powerless to help, the Guides commenced their retirement. With the great mountains as an amphitheatre the drama began to unfold itself before the gaze of waiting thousands. At first so far away were they, so few, so scattered, and clad to match the colour of the hills, that only the strongest glasses could make out the position of the Guides; but apparent to the naked eye of all was the great straggling mass which was falling with relentless swiftness, guillotine-like, on the narrow neck of the communications with the bridge. With cool intrepid courage, with a deliberation which appeared almost exasperating to the onlookers, Colonel Battye and his men took up the challenge. Little parties of soldiers could be descried slowly sauntering back, a few yards only, then disappearing amongst the rocks with a rattle of rifle-fire. Then back came more little parties of soldiers, all seemingly sauntering, all with the long sunny day before them. And after them bounded great waves of men in blue, and men in white, only to break and stagger back before those little clumps of rock in which the rearmost soldiers lay. "Get back, get back! Damn you, why don't you get back?" shouted the spectators on the eastern bank in impotent excitement. But no word of this reached the Guides on the slopes of the still far-off mountain-side; nor would they have heeded had they heard, for they had been born and bred to the two simple maxims, "Be fiery quick in attack, but deadly slow in retirement." And so slowly back they came, and in their wake lay strewn the white and blue figures, all huddled up, or stark and flat.

The retirement now brought the regiment down the spur of a lofty hill which forms the angle where the Jandul River flows into the Panjkora. This hill is to the south of the Jandul, while the bridge-head was to the north. Thus to reach their entrenchment the Guides had to retire down the spur they were now on, and to cross the Jandul.

It was now noon, and at about this time the enemy's masses were seen to divide in two; one-half keeping to the right, so as to support the attack on the Guides, while the other column continued down the Jandul, so as to cut the regiment off from its bridge-head. Foot by foot (to the spectators it seemed inch by inch) the different companies retired alternatively, fiercely assailed on all hands, yet coolly firing volley after volley, relinquishing quietly and almost imperceptibly one strong position, only to take up another a few yards back.

At last the impatient spectators on the left bank of the Panjkora had a chance of helping, for the enemy were now within range of the mountain-guns, and the steady and accurate fire of these greatly relieved the pressure. At the same time the two companies of the Guides in the entrenchment, seeing that the enemy's left column was closing down, moved out to check their advance, and to stretch out to the rest of the regiment a helping hand. The whole of the 2nd Brigade also lined their bank of the Panjkora, and prepared with flank fire to help the Guides, when they reached the foot of the spur. Here it would have to cross several hundred yards of level ground, on which the green barley was standing waist-high, ford the Jandul, about three feet deep, and then across more open fields to the friendly bridge-head. This naturally was the most difficult part of the operation, and in executing it Colonel Fred Battye, the fourth of the heroic brothers to be killed in action, fell mortally wounded. He was, as might be expected from one of his race, always at the point of danger throughout the retirement, and as he crossed the open zone among the last, a sharp-shooter at close range, from behind a withered tree, fired the fatal shot.

It was on this open ground that the extraordinary bravery of the enemy was most brilliantly shown. Standard-bearers with reckless gallantry could be seen rushing to certain destruction, falling perhaps within ten yards of the line of the Guides; men, who had used up all their ammunition, would rush forward with large rocks and hurl them at the soldiers, courting instant death. Nothing could damp their ardour, or check the fury of their assaults. Even after the Guides had crossed the river, and the enemy were under a severe flank fire from the Gordon Highlanders and King's Own Scottish Borderers, they dashed into the stream, where each man stood out as clear as a bullseye on a target, and attempted to close again. But not a man got across, so steady and well directed was the flank fire of the British regiments. This welcome diversion enabled the Guides to complete the retirement into their entrenchment at the bridge-head, and there make rapid preparation for the attack that must follow; for though the enemy had lost six hundred men, their spirit was by no means broken.

Reinforcements consisting of two companies of the 4th Sikhs, and the Devonshire Regiment Maxim gun, were sent across after much labour by means of a little skin raft that only held two at a time. The near bank was also sungared and held by the 2nd Brigade and the Derajat mountain battery, which at eight hundred yards' range could fire over the heads of those at the bridge-head. Several officers of the Guides' cavalry also volunteered to cross over and help their comrades, for in a night attack it was a matter of holding their own, covering fire from the near bank being too dangerous an expedient.

The Guides, who were now under that good and cheery soldier Fred. Campbell, put out no picquets, so as to keep clear the field of fire, and every man slept, or sat awake, at his fighting station with his rifle in his hand. The enemy could be heard close by in large numbers, hidden by a fold in the ground, and directly darkness set in they began yelling and tom-tomming in the most approved fashion. This was to work up any flagging spirits that there might be, and to exalt the courage of all, for two thousand chosen warriors, sword in hand, lay ready in the standing corn, to make a desperate dash at the given signal, which was to be the first peep of the crescent moon over the mountains, calculated for about midnight. There was some warlike cunning in this, for when a moon is about to rise every weary watcher is looking for it during the last moments, and then looking down again would find everything dark as the pit's mouth by comparison. In those few seconds the assailants meant to bound across the short intervening space, and come to close grips with the enemy who had staved them off all day and half the night.

It was then that the use of one of the resources of science stood the British in good stead, and probably saved the lives of many hundreds. The officer commanding the Derajat battery, peering anxiously through the darkness, and perplexed to know what was happening, bethought him to throw a star shell over the Guides' entrenchment, so as to light up the ground beyond. The effect was magical. "What new devilment is this?" exclaimed the brave but ignorant tribesmen. And when another, and yet another, came, they said: "This is an invention of the Evil One; it is magic, and will cast a spell over us. We cannot fight against devils such as these."

And so those few harmless fireworks effected the same purpose as a storm of shot and shell. All that vast throng melted away, and only a few of the braver sort held post till morning. But before going they inflicted one great loss, mortally wounding the gifted Captain Peebles, the only officer who knew the working of a Maxim gun, then new to the army.

The remainder of the campaign was a matter of a few days. How Kelly, with his gallant regiment, the 32nd Pioneers, pushed on from the north, overcoming stupendous difficulties; how a strong force of levies under the Khan of

Dir was thrust on from the south; how Aylmer, the brave and resourceful Sapper, working night and day threw a suspension bridge of telegraph wire across the Panjkora; how Sir Robert Low, crossing with his whole force, fought a decisive and conclusive battle at Mundah; and how thus, by a fine strategic combination, worked from widely divergent bases, Sir George White effected in the course of seventeen days the relief of the sore beset garrison of Chitral, are recorded amongst the many and sterling achievements of the army of India.

Amongst the trophies and standards brought down by the Guides was a solid brass cannon of tremendous weight captured at Mundah. In a mountainous country where there are no roads, and for a weight far beyond the carrying capacity of a pack animal, there appeared to be no alternative to leaving the gun behind. But rather than do this the men volunteered to carry it themselves, and thus twenty men at a time carried the gun while their comrades carried a double load of arms and ammunition. The gun now stands at Mardan near the memorial to the officers and men who fell in defence of the Kabul Embassy, and on it is engraved in Persian the curious and bombastic inscription:--

>   It's mouth is open wide to eat. What shall I call it? A gun or a serpent? This gun is most heavy, and makes victory certain. There is none like it in India or Kabul. Made by Ghulam Rasul.

## Chapter 13
# The Malakand, 1897

As the officers of the Guides were sitting at dinner on the night of July 26th, 1897, a telegram was handed to Colonel Adams informing him that the Malakand position had been attacked by overwhelming numbers, that the garrison was with difficulty holding its own, and asking him to bring up his corps as speedily as possible to its succour.

Accustomed for decades to these sudden appeals, the Guides' cavalry, bag and baggage, supplies, transport, and all complete, were off in three hours, and the Guides' infantry followed them. The march was twenty-nine miles along the flat to Dargai, and then seven miles rise and two thousand feet climb to the summit of the Malakand Pass. For cavalry, considering the time of year, it was by no means a mean undertaking; for infantry it was one of the highest achievement. To march thirty-six miles under service conditions, in the most favourable circumstances of weather, temperature, and training, is a high test of endurance; but to do so when the muscles are enervated with heat, along a treeless, waterless road, during the fiercest term of the summer solstice, was a feat to secure the admiration of every soldier. The march was accomplished in sixteen hours, the first twenty-nine miles being covered without any regular halt, and the last seven miles up a mountain on which the blazing afternoon sun was beating its fiercest. Yet not a man fell out, and it is recorded by an eye-witness[24] that as the regiment

---

24. The Story of the Malakand Field Force; by Winston Spencer Churchill, Lieut. 4th Hussars. London, 1898.

passed the quarter-guards, the men came to attention, and answered the salute as smartly as if just returning from a parade march. The Guides of 1897 had borne themselves no wit less worthily than the Guides of 1857 or the Guides of 1879. To Lieutenant P. Eliott-Lockhart belongs the honour of commanding the Guides' infantry in this fine soldierly performance, and the Distinguished Service Order worthily decorated him for this and other gallant service. To arrive as a reinforcement is to be welcome enough; to arrive by exertions beyond the compass of calculation, in time to afford assistance at the critical moment, is the fortune of few. Yet thrice has this good fortune smiled on the efforts of the Guides, at Delhi, at Kabul, and at the Malakand.

Arrived, and without a moment to rest or ease their belts, these weary, but stout-hearted fellows went straight on outpost duty, that 27th of July, 1897, and spent the livelong night, not in sleep, or even a quiet turn of sentry-go, but in a desperate hand to hand fight with swarms of brave and persistent warriors.

Piece by piece the officers heard the strange story of the sudden rising. It appears that while the officers of the Malakand garrison, in days of profound peace, were playing polo down at Khar, a village three miles away, the villagers came to them with a warning. They said that a very holy mullah from Upper Swat was coming down the valley with a large following to attack the Malakand, and advised the officers to get back to their defences as soon as possible; they even assisted back the grooms with the spare ponies. Yet these very same friendly villagers a few hours later were caught in the frenzied flame of fanaticism, and were charging with the most devoted bravery breastworks held by troops commanded by the very officers whom they had just helped to save.

Amongst the officers playing polo were Lieutenants Rattray and Minchin, who belonged to the garrison of Chakdara some seven or eight miles up the Swat Valley. To return

THIRTY-FOUR WEARERS OF THE STAR FOR VALOUR, ALL SERVING AT ONE TIME IN THE CORPS OF GUIDES. THIS IS THE HIGHEST DISTINCTION OPEN TO AN INDIAN SOLDIER FOR GALLANTRY IN ACTION.

to their posts they had therefore to pass right through the tide of armed men flowing down the valley in great numbers. Yet as illustrating the chivalrous nature of the wild hillmen, a trait somewhat unusual amongst the more fanatical Pathans, the officers were allowed to pass unmolested, and indeed here and there a friendly voice bade them make good speed home. The British officer's custom of being out and about doing something, instead of sitting permanently at home studying or playing chess, stood him in good stead on this occasion, giving, as it proved, a good four hours' warning in advance.

It was not till after ten o'clock at night that the carefully planned attacks on the Malakand and Chakdara were delivered simultaneously by great swarms of tribesmen, with a resolution and bravery worthy of the highest admiration. At the Malakand there were many anxious moments, for the position was an extended one, and, by the nature of the ground, difficult for a small garrison to preserve from penetration. It was a night of individual heroism, a soldier's battle, where little knots of men under their officers fought independently, and with undiminished courage, though often cut off from all communication. No less brave was the enemy, and it was not until dawn that he reluctantly withdrew. This was the first of five nights and days through which the British garrison had to stand this stern ordeal.

The first thing to be done when daylight made concerted movements possible, was to contract the perimeter of defence, so as to make it more tenable by the number of troops available. The original garrison was now augmented by the arrival of the Guides, horse and foot. It was with considerable reluctance that Colonel Meiklejohn, who had himself been wounded by a sword-cut, decided on abandoning what was known as the North Camp, a position some distance below and isolated from the Malakand. This camp had been established both to allow the cavalry and pack-animals to be near water, of which there was scarcity on the Malakand itself; and also for sanitary reasons, so as to keep so large a number of animals out of a restricted area. The abandonment of this camp, necessary though it was, undoubtedly had an extraordinarily heartening effect on the enemy. All night they had fought desperately, and lost heavily, without apparently gaining any result; but the retirement of the troops from the North Camp, besides leaving in their hands the large tents and heavy baggage of all sorts, impossible to move at short notice, showed that the garrison also had felt the stress of battle.

Strongly reinforced, and with new heart, so soon as night fell the tribesmen renewed their attack. As illustrating the desperate nature of the fighting, out of one picquet of twenty-five men of the 31st Punjab Infantry, the native officer and eighteen men were killed or wounded; while out of another picquet, consisting of the Guides and forty-five Sikhs, twenty-one were killed or wounded; and all this was done in close hand to hand fighting. Lieutenant Lockhart thus describes the scene:

> It was a veritable pandemonium that would seem to have been let loose around us. Bands of ghazis, worked up by their religious enthusiasm into a frenzy of fanatical excitement, would charge our breastworks again and again, leaving their dead in scores after each repulse, while those of their comrades who were unarmed would encourage their efforts by shouting, with much beating of tom-toms, and other musical instruments. Amidst the discordant din which raged around, we could even distinguish bugle calls, evidently sounded by some disant bugler of our native army. As he suddenly collapsed in the middle of the "officers' mess call" we concluded that a bullet had brought him to an untimely end.[25]

---

25. A Frontier Campaign; by the Viscount Fincastle, V.C., Lieutenant 16th Lancers, and P.C. Eliott-Lockhart, D.S.O., Lieutenant Queen's Own Corps of Guides. London, 1898.

The fighting went on all night, and at daybreak the garrison, to show that they were none the worse for it, made a spirited counter attack, the 24th Punjab Infantry under Lieutenant Climo, the senior surviving officer, doing great execution. A desultory fire was kept up by the enemy during the day, while the British force improved their defences.

As darkness fell on the third night, the enemy, undaunted and heavily reinforced from countries as far afield as Buner, again advanced to the attack, the brunt of which fell on the 31st Punjab Infantry, a regiment so depleted by losses that Lieutenant H. Maclean, of the Guides' cavalry, was requisitioned to give a helping hand. This officer, together with Lieutenants Ford and Swinley, were severely wounded. Towards morning the attack again died away, and the indomitable garrison still held its own.

On the fourth night, in addition to bonfires placed out in front of the defences, to make the enemy's movements clear, it was decided to try the effect of mines, and portions of a serai, lately occupied by the Sappers and now abandoned, were accordingly undermined. At nightfall the enemy immediately seized this serai as an advance post to further their attack, and when it was crowded the mine was fired with fatal results. For a time a death-like silence reigned, the enemy being apparently thunderstruck at the awful disaster. Minor attacks, however, were still persisted in, and the tribesmen did not draw off till three in the morning.

A fifth night had barely settled down on the garrison when, undeterred by four unsuccessful and costly attacks, or by the terrors of unseen mines, the enemy again swarmed down on the weary but undismayed defenders. To add to their difficulties, a severe dust storm, followed by torrents of rain, fell on the camp, and at the height of the storm a most determined attack was made on the 45th Sikhs, but was repulsed with great loss. Sitting drenched to the skin the garrison patiently awaited the dawn.

That day, the 31st of July, brought welcome reinforcements, consisting of the 35th Sikhs and the 38th Dogras, under Colonel Reid. Thus strengthened, Colonel Meiklejohn determined to take the offensive, and attempt to force his way to the assistance of the isolated garrison of Chakdara. The cavalry, consisting of the Guides and 11th Bengal Lancers, were to lead the way, but these regiments before they could get into the open were so strongly attacked in the rocky defiles from which they tried to issue, that they could make no headway and had to return to camp.

Meanwhile Sir Bindon Blood had arrived to take over the command, and decided to postpone further endeavours to relieve Chakdara till the next day. The intervening night seems to have been a quiet one, and before dawn the British force commenced to move. The attack was unexpected at so early an hour: the enemy were surprised and driven out from the heights to the east of the Malakand position; and the command of ground thus gained enabled this successful column to clear the flank of the exit from the Malakand, and to ensure the unopposed initial advance of the main body. Before reaching the open valley, however, strong parties of the enemy were found holding the rocky spurs and kopjes intervening. These after sharp fighting were carried with the bayonet by the Guides, 35th and 45th Sikhs, and the way was opened, the cavalry doing great execution amongst the flying enemy.

Meanwhile the small garrison of Chakdara had, for the space of six days and nights, been undergoing no mean adventures. It will be remembered that Lieutenants Rattray and Minchin (the Political Officer) were, on the afternoon of July 26th, playing polo at Khar, some seven or eight miles away down the Swat Valley. Warned there of impending trouble they rode back through the gathering storm to their post, the little fort of Chakdara situated on the north bank of the Swat River. Soon after ten o'clock that night a beacon, lighted by a friendly hand across the valley, gave timely notice that an attack was imminent. The garrison, two companies of the 45th Sikhs and twenty men of the 11th Bengal Lancers, hurried to their posts, and after a short delay the assault began, and never ceased for the best part of a week!

The fort was badly situated for defence, being indeed more a bridge-head guard than a fort. The rock on which it stood was commanded by a great spur running down to it from the west; and the only obstacle that prevented that spur being occupied in full by the enemy was a small tower, used for signalling purposes and occupied by a few Sikhs. The story of that little post is an epic in itself; surrounded on all sides, isolated from all help, with scanty food, and at the end no water, for six days and nights it gallantly held its own.

As for the fort itself, it was so completely commanded by the fire from the spurs that to move about in it was to court death. Yet thus glued to the walls, and assailed night and day by brave warriors whose numbers rose rapidly from fifteen hundred to over ten thousand, a few young British officers with a couple of hundred Sikhs again and again rolled back the tide of war. The history of that week was as the history of the Malakand, continuous attacks by night and day; but the execution done on the enemy, considering the smallness of the garrison, was comparatively higher; statistics are difficult to gather, but a fairly accurate estimate puts their loss at two thousand. And, to illustrate the indomitable courage and unflagging spirit with which the defence was maintained to the end, when on the last day the thrice welcome sight of the Guides' cavalry and the 11th Bengal Lancers, coming over the Amandara Pass, met the view of that weary little band, they in their turn became the attackers, and, led by the undaunted Rattray, sallied forth and stormed the enemy's positions. To Hedley Wright who commanded, and to Rattray and Wheatley who were the soul of the defence, as well as to the gallant Sikhs, is due the admiration of every soldier who loves to hear of a good fight fought out to the end as British officers and men led by them know how to fight it.

As at the Malakand, so at Chakdara, and so times without number, it is the gallant British subaltern, in spite of silly chatter, who again and again has shown the highest attributes of an officer and a soldier. It is the foolish custom of a certain class of Englishman to decry all that is their own; and amongst the latest of these victims of a dyspeptic imagination is the British officer. Men call him stupid, who would themselves have no chance of passing the intellectual test which every young officer has to go through. Sitting safe and smug at home they libel the courage and devotion of the gallant gentleman who is giving his life for them. Perhaps against these may be placed the word of an old soldier, who for thirty years has seen the British officer, as fighter, diplomatist, and administrator, in all parts of the world, and who has not lightly come to the conclusion that he has not his better in the army of any country, and is only equalled by his brother of the British Navy.

\* \* \* \* \*

Marshalling and redistributing his forces, Sir Bindon Blood, after the relief of Chakdara, proceeded systematically to punish the tribes involved in the late fanatical upheaval. Amongst the first to be so dealt with were the tribesmen of the Upper Swat, and the action of Landaki was the result.

The tribesmen held a position on a big spur running down from the mountains, and meeting an unfordable river with a steep cliff. Round the face of this cliff a narrow causeway led to a fairly open valley beyond. It was the business of the infantry to clear this spur, or ridge, and this they accomplished after some severe climbing and hard fighting. As the defeated enemy were seen streaming across the valley, making for a further ridge two or three miles in the rear, the Guides' cavalry were let loose in pursuit; but before debouching into the valley they had to pass along the causeway, some three-quarters of a mile in length, in single file. As everyone knows, who has experience of single file work, even a moderate pace in front means inevitable straggling behind. The officer leading, in his eagerness to get at the enemy, lost sight of this fact, and so soon as he made the valley, with the first few men set off at a round pace after the enemy. At the head of the pursuit was also Lieutenant R.T. Greaves, of the Lancashire Fusiliers, who was acting as war-correspondent to a newspaper. After traversing a mile, and leaving the men further and further behind, the two officers saw the enemy passing through a wooded graveyard and on to a spur some eighty yards in the rear.

Colonel Adams, who was coming up fast with the main body, shouted to the two officers to stop, but owing to the noise of firing could not make himself heard. He at once saw that the place to seize was the graveyard, cavalry pursuit up a rocky hill being naturally impracticable, and from there to open fire on the retreating enemy. He therefore at once seized the graveyard with dismounted men. To describe the events of the next few minutes it had best be done in the words of an officer who was an eye-witness and whose account appears in A Frontier Campaign:

> On Palmer and Greaves approaching the hill, they were subject to a heavy fire from the enemy. Palmer's horse was at once killed, whilst Greaves, having been shot at close quarters, fell, some twenty yards further on, among the Pathans, who at once proceeded to hack at him with their swords. Seeing this, Adams and Fincastle went out to his assistance followed by two sowars, who galloped towards Palmer, at that moment engaged in hand-to-hand conflict with a standard-bearer. Palmer had been shot through the right wrist

*and was only saved by the opportune appearance of these two men, who enabled him to get back to the shelter of the ziarat in safety. Meanwhile Fincastle, who had had his horse killed while galloping up to where Greaves lay, tried to lift Greaves on to Adams's horse, in the process of which Greaves was again shot through the body, and Adams's horse wounded. They were soon joined by the two sowars who had been to Palmer's assistance, and almost immediately after by Maclean, who having first dismounted his squadron in the ziarat, had very pluckily ridden out with four of his men to the assistance of this small party, who otherwise would have been rushed by the enemy. With his assistance Greaves was successfully brought in, but unfortunately Maclean, who had dismounted in order to help in lifting the body on to his horse, was shot through both thighs and died almost immediately.*

Of the survivors Colonel Adams and Lord Fincastle received the Victoria Cross for their valour on this occasion; while ten years after, as a graceful tribute to the heroism of the dead, the Victoria Cross was also bestowed on Hector Maclean, and sent to his family. As Lord Fincastle was attached to the Guides during the campaign the probably unique historic record was established of three officers in one regiment earning the Victoria Cross on the same day. Nor were the men forgotten, all those who had shown conspicuous gallantry being decorated with the Order of Merit.

## Chapter 14
# The Home of the Guides

When the Guides about the middle of the last century first pitched their wandering tents in the plains of Yusafzai they were only birds of passage, in hot pursuit of some band of marauders, or swiftly marching to surprise a distant stronghold. But as the border became more settled, and sudden movements were less seldom called for, a position was chosen within striking distance of all the centres of disturbance. And thus came to be selected the site of the little cantonment, which since has sent forth generations of steel-bred warriors to keep bright the ancient flame; a small oasis, rescued by rough but kindly hands from the dry and desolate desert, and which the leisure of sixty years has served to turn into the beautiful and cherished home of the Guides.

The camp in due course shed its white wings and became a dust-hued fort. As seen by an eagle soaring overhead, its shape is that of a five-pointed star, and on four of the points stood the officers' quarters, while on the fifth were the magazine and place d'armes. All round the inside of the star, tucked away under the parapets, were the rude shelters of the infantry, while a hornwork held the troops of cavalry. For a few hundred yards round the jungle and scrub were cleared away, a Union Jack run up to the modest mast-head on the keep, and Hôti-Mardan Fort became not only the home of the Guides, but also the symbol of British power on the wild borders of Yaghistan, the land of everlasting conflict and of unending vendettas.

It was the pride of a far-distant generation to name the bastions of the old fort after famous leaders who had gone before: Lumsden, the genial dashing soldier, who stamped his type on the small beginnings; Hodson, the far-famed leader of light horse; Daly, whose steadfast resolve carried through the great march to Delhi; Sam Browne, the one-armed hero of a hundred fights.

Soon after the Mutiny the fort began to overflow, for the country was now getting more settled, and British officers could venture to build houses outside the walls of fortified enclosures. Thus the Assistant-Commissioner migrated eight hundred yards to the south-east, while an officers' mess was built on the river bank two hundred yards to the north-west. A quarter of a century passed before more houses were added, and then at intervals of a few years came the church and more houses, while extensions of the soldiers' lines took place to accommodate the increasing numbers.

And thus it stands to-day, the little five-bastioned fort, round which are loosely thrown half a dozen houses and a church. And yet there is a difference, for the picture is now set, not in dull desert tints, but in soft shades of green. Everywhere are avenues and clumps of great trees, hedges of roses, of limes, and deronta encircle every garden, the green of the polo grounds is as that of the Emerald Isle. Even the old fort has lost its grimness, and the mud walls have given place to beautiful terraces bright with every flower; while the once formidable moat is spanned by peaceful rustic bridges, clustered thick with climbing roses, and giving access to the gardens and orchards which spread along the glacis.

On the Hodson bastion stands the old mess, now an officers' quarter, where in bygone stormy days they used to sit at dinner with revolvers handy, and swords stacked in the corner, alert and ready for sudden alarm or excursion. A strange imprint of those old times remained for many years, a bullet-mark high up in one corner of the dining-room; and this bullet, according to tradition, was fired at dinner by Sir Sam Browne, who was a deadly shot, and nailed to the wall the tail of a cobra which was disappearing into a crevice.

Passing near the Hodson bastion and running to the present mess is Godby-road, named after General C.J. Godby, who after nearly losing his head from a sabre stroke in the Sikh War, again well-nigh lost it near this spot at the hands of a ghazi. The incident affords an early instance of the ready resource which has always been one of the typical characteristics of the Guides. When Godby was cut down by a treacherous blow there happened to be two or three men within hail, and these at once dashed to the rescue; but they were disarmed, while the fanatic brandished a razor-edged Afghan blade, and was prepared to sell his life dearly. Sharp eyes and ready wit, however, came to aid. Close by was a tent pitched, the guy ropes tied to long heavy wooden pegs such as are used in India. As quick as thought the tent was struck, the pegs wrenched from the ground, and the ghazi surrounded, overpowered, secured, and incidentally in due course hanged.

The present mess is full not only of historical mementoes, as is only natural, but also of archæological treasures of great value and antiquity. On the walls captured banners, swords and daggers, guns and pistols, share the honours with portraits of old commanders and of the mighty dead with their swords beneath them. Over the anteroom mantelpiece is a very gracious picture of Queen Victoria, presented by her Majesty in 1876; and this is flanked by pictures of King Edward the Seventh, who is Colonel-in-Chief of the corps, and Queen Alexandra, both presented by their Majesties when they were Prince and Princess of Wales. Over the mantelpiece in the dining-room is an excellent oil painting of Sir Harry Lumsden, who raised the corps.

One of the most interesting relics is one leaf of a mahogany table, captured at the siege of Delhi and used in camp on the Ridge; the other two leaves were taken by the 60th Rifles and the 2nd Gurkhas, who lay alongside the Guides at Hindu Rao's house. On the leaves are roughly carved symbolic crests and mottoes for the three regiments: A Maltese Cross and *Celer et Audax* for the 60th Rifles; crossed swords and *Stout and Steady* for the Gurkhas; and crossed Afghan knives with *Rough and Ready* for the Guides. On this latter leaf may be seen standing a cigar-lighter made out of grapeshot picked up in camp during the siege.

High up on the walls all round are endless trophies of the chase, probably the finest collection in Asia--Ovis poli, Ovis Ammon, Ibex, markhor, bara sing, and bison; besides specimens from other continents whither officers have gone in pursuit of sport or war. A splendid collection of plate testifies to success in many a field of sport, polo, tent-pegging, and shooting.

The archæological treasures consist of sculptures and friezes of Greco-Buddhist origin, illustrating incidents in the life of Buddha, while the statues represent the great Gautama and some of his disciples. Most of these are still in perfect preservation, though varying from fifteen hundred to two thousand years in antiquity. They were all discovered, many years ago, within a few miles of the mess, and are naturally preserved with the greatest care. Savants from even so far afield as France, Germany, and America have journeyed to see them.

The mess stands in a five-acre garden, which has been the joy of many generations; for, apart from its abundant fertility, amidst its shades are to be found a swimming-bath and racquet-court, as well as tennis, badminton, and croquet lawns. Oranges, strawberries, peaches, plums, apricots, grapes, loquats and other fruits flourish and abound, while

The old Graveyard at Mardan

nearly every species of English flower and vegetable grows strong and well. Great trees give shade and peace to the place. But perhaps the greatest attraction to the hot and weary officer, and which leaves the most grateful memory with the dusky warriors who march through in war and peace, is the deep cool swimming-bath alongside which under the trees is spread a breakfast that suits the hour and climate. There are perhaps few more grateful feelings than on a summer's morning to come out of the fierce heat and dust and glare of field-exercises, or a march from the Malakand or Nowshera, and to find oneself in these cool and comforting surroundings.

Just outside the garden is the old graveyard, where rest in God the brave hearts who have fought the good fight, and now with sword in sheath watch with kindly pride the keen young blades who follow in their steps. Side by side lie two of the heroic Battyes, Wigram and Fred, two of the four brothers who died for their Queen and Country. As has been related elsewhere, Wigram was killed in 1879 while charging at the head of his squadron at Futtehabad in Afghanistan, and Fred fell mortally wounded just as he had completed a most brilliant operation at the Panjkora river, on the march to the relief of Chitral in 1895. Close to them lies that kindly, upright gentleman, beloved of all, Bob Hutchinson, who fell at the head of the Guides during a night attack on the border village of Malandrai in 1886. A few yards in another direction may be seen a stone to the memory of A.M. Ommanney, a young officer who was assassinated by a fanatic in mistake for his brother. Besides these, and many other single graves, there are large inclusive monuments to the memory of the officers and men of various regiments who have fought on these borders. Amongst them may be seen those erected to the memory of the officers and men of the 71st Highland Light Infantry,

93rd Sutherland Highlanders, and 101st Royal Bengal Fusiliers, all killed in the Umbeyla campaign of 1863.

Outside the old graveyard, standing at the meeting of three roads, is a very fine mulberry tree, planted at the spot where, according to old soldiers, Colonel Spottiswoode, of the 55th Native Infantry, in deep distress at the mutiny of his regiment, determined to take his own life rather than live to see it disgraced, and under which, according to tradition, he lies buried.

Passing through the bazaar, we come to the Memorial arch and tank, erected by Government to Major Sir Louis Cavignari, Mr. W. Jenkyns, Lieutenant Walter Hamilton, V.C., Surgeon Kelly and the native officers, non-commissioned-officers, and men of the Guides who fell in the defence of the Kabul Residency, September, 3rd, 1879. Just outside the memorial garden is the spot where Lieutenant A.M. Ommanney was assassinated, now known as the Ommanney cross-roads.

Every road in the cantonment has a name, and each name in itself is an honoured memory. Some bear the names of old officers of the corps, while others keep green the memory of those fallen in war. Amongst the former will be found Sir Alfred Wilde, Sir Charles Keyes, Sir Frances Jenkins, and Sir John McQueen. Sir Alfred Wilde commanded the corps with great distinction during the Umbeyla campaign of 1863, and afterwards went on to command the Punjab Frontier Force, as did also Sir Charles Keyes. Of Sir Frances Jenkins a book might be written, for his connection with the Guides extended over nearly twenty-four years. He was one of the most accomplished soldiers who have ever served in the Indian Army and carried with him much of the breezy skill in war of Sir Harry Lumsden. Sir John McQueen also was a soldier of great renown, who afterwards commanded the Punjab Frontier Force. Other roads bear the names of Bob Hutchinson, who, as above recorded, was killed in the night attack on Malandrai; Walter Hamilton, killed in defence of the Kabul Residency; Hector MacLean, who earned the Victoria Cross and died to save a comrade at Landaki, in Swat; Quentin Battye, who, mortally wounded, passed peacefully away at Delhi with the words *'Dulce et decorum est pro patria mori'* on his lips; Wigram Battye, killed bravely charging in Afghanistan, and Fred Battye, killed at the Panjkora. Great names these all, and spreading still their soldier influence, perhaps insensibly, over the spirit of their old home and regiment.

Out beyond the cavalry parade-ground is the Home Farm, and on each side of it run the cavalry and infantry rifle-ranges, skirted by fine avenues of trees. Between the infantry range and the church are two of the best polo-grounds in India,--grounds which have produced many famous players and many famous teams. The church was erected by public subscription to the memory of Colonel Hutchinson, and claims the great attraction to sojourners in a foreign land of being like a little English church. On the walls are tablets to the memory of Sir Harry Lumsden; Major F.H. Barton, the cheery, gallant sportsman who was killed at polo in 1902; Major Gaikskill; A.W. Wilde, son of Sir Alfred; Hector MacLean; Quentin and Fred Battye; Major G.H. Bretherton, who was drowned on the way to Lhassa; Charlie Keyes, son of Sir Charles, treacherously killed in West Africa, and many others. The churchyard is beautifully laid out with many rare plants, flowers, and trees. There remains only, to finish up with, the old cricket-ground, now used entirely for lawn-tennis, badminton, and croquet; for cricket flourishes not in India at this day, though doubtless a revival may come before many years, as is so often the case with games.

The daily life at Mardan is much the same as in any other

Indian cantonment. In the early morning comes parade or manoeuvre, growing painfully early as the brief hot weather creeps on. Stables follow for the cavalry, and work in the lines for the infantry. Next comes orderly-room for the adjutants and others; and twice a week durbar. The durbar in an Indian regiment takes the place of the formal orderly-room of a British regiment. It is held in the open, under the trees, or at any convenient spot; and the underlying principle is that any man in the regiment may be present to hear, and, when called upon, to speak. It is a sort of open court, whereat not only are delinquents brought up for judgment, but all matters connected with the welfare of the men, and especially such as in any way touch their pockets or privileges, are openly discussed. To add to the semi-informal and friendly nature of the assembly, all the men are allowed to wear plain clothes.

In the afternoon both officers and men are, as a rule, free to amuse themselves with such sport and games as may seem good to them. Round and about Mardan there is fairly good small-game shooting, the game-book in a good year showing over three thousand head shot by the officers. Amongst these are wild duck of many varieties, wild geese, snipe, partridges, hare, and quail.

The ancient and royal sport of falconry, which long flourished, has of late years become much restricted owing to the increase of cultivation. One of the highest forms of falconry, and one little known in other countries, was the pursuit of the ravine deer. Only falcons reared from the nest could be trained to this sport, and they had to be obtained from far off Central Asia. The falcon used was the Cherug, or Saker as she is known in Europe, and the method of training is interesting. From the nest upwards the bird was taught that the only possible place to obtain food was from between a pair of antlers. At first fed sitting between them, as she learnt

THE CHURCH AT MARDAN

to flutter she was encouraged to bridge a short gap to her dinner. Then, as she grew stronger, she flew short distances to get her food as before. The next step was the use of a stuffed deer on wheels, which, when the hawk was loosed, was run along, and thus accustomed her to the idea of movement in getting her food. At the same time she was accustomed to the presence of greyhounds, for without the aid of these she would never be able to bring down her quarry. For the Pathan saying is: "The first day a ravine deer is born a fleet man may catch it; the second day a dog; and the third day no one!"

The hawks, which were flown in pairs, were now taken into the field, keen set, to use a term in falconry; that is very hungry, but not weakened or disheartened by hunger. Directly a herd of deer was sighted the hawks were cast loose, and, soaring up, soon descried a seemingly familiar object with a pair of antlers, between which there was doubtless a delicious meal. Off, therefore, they went straight for the quarry, and, stooping, struck for the deer's antlers. Naturally, however, no bird of that size could bring a deer to earth, or even stop him unaided; but the hawks had done their initial work, and the riders, with a couple of greyhounds leashed to the stirrup, rode hard for the spot where the hawks were striking, and let slip the hounds.

The rattle of hoofs at once stampeded the deer, and then the chase began. The hawks, in turn towering and stooping, showed the line to take, for the deer was invisible to the dogs, and generally to the riders. But the dogs had learnt to work by the hawks, and cutting a corner here, or favoured by a jink there, gradually closed up, the part of the hawks being, by constant striking, to delay and confuse the deer. It was a hard ride and a fine combination which secured the quarry, and, as with all sport worth the name, it was even chances on the deer. When the combination failed and the deer got away, it was a bit of human nature to see the meeting between the hawks and the dogs. The hawks would be sitting on the ground or on a bush, evidently and unmistakably using language of the most sulphurous nature; while the dogs came up, their tongues out, their tails between their legs, and with a general air of exhaustion, dejection, and apology. As they slunk up the muttered curses broke forth: "You! you lazy hound! Call yourself a greyhound! You're a fat-tailed sheep, that's what you are, nothing more!" And up would get friend hawk and cuff and strike and harry that poor dog, till he fairly yelped and fled to his master for protection.

Duck and bustard still afford sport to the falconer, but he has to work further afield, and gets less in return than in the olden times. The bustard gives good sport, and often a good run of three or four miles; indeed there is on record a case of an eleven mile point.

On the mountain range which lies close to Mardan markhor are to be found, and some good heads have been shot; while in the lower slopes good bags of chikore, black and grey partridge, and rock-pigeons may be obtained. There are two of the best polo-grounds in India, and the Guides can generally put up a good team or two to compete in the various tournaments, and generally one or more challenge-cups are to be seen on their mess table. Racquets, tennis, and hockey, lime-cutting, tent-pegging and other mounted sports are also part of the weekly life; while friendly visits, given and taken, keep touch with the neighbouring stations.

The climate of these parts is on the whole eminently healthy and bracing. True, there are four months of very hot weather, but they get lost sight of in the keen delight of the other eight. Red cheeks with buoyant activity and spirits carry their own advertisement.

Thus, briefly described, has been the home of the Guides

for upwards of sixty years; a little kingdom barely a mile square, but full of happy associations for all who have lived there. It is a quiet, unassuming spot, which year by year has bred, and sent forth to fight, many a gallant officer and brave soldier; and which in future years hopes to keep bright the shining record of great deeds that have gone before.

# Recollections of the Indian Mutiny

By Gunner MacCallam

*Royal Artillery*

from the Leonaur book
**Tommy Atkins' War Stories**
Fourteen first hand accounts from the ranks of the British Army during Queen Victoria's Empire

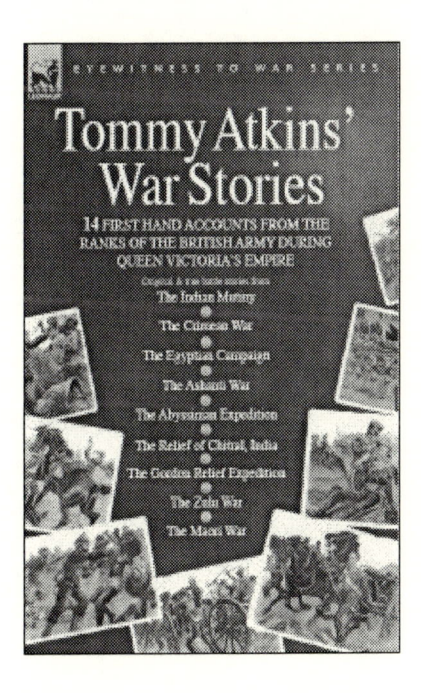

# Recollections of the Indian Mutiny

I enlisted in 1852, in the Royal Artillery, then stationed at Woolwich, and six months afterwards went out to India, where, after spending some few years at various stations, I found myself in 1857 at Meerut, with a regiment of infantry, one of dragoons, and a troop and battery of artillery, numbering altogether one thousand seven hundred and seventeen men, under the command of Major-General Hewitt.

There were also two regiments of native infantry and one of light cavalry, numbering in all two thousand seven hundred, and these men, with others, had been pretty mutinous. I remember, on the 6th of May, cartridges, made especially for the purpose of satisfying their religious scruples, were offered to the native cavalry, but eighty-five troopers refused to accept them, and they were tried by court-martial, and sentenced to various terms of imprisonment extending from five to ten years. On the 9th they were put in irons, and conducted to prison under a guard of Sepoys. We were posted at a distance of three miles from the native camp.

On the following day, which was Sunday, at about five o'clock in the afternoon, the native regiments rose in mutiny, fired on their officers, rushed to the prison, rescued the mutineers and upwards of a thousand convicts confined there, and set the building on fire.

English people were killed wherever they could be found. Bungalows were blazing in all directions, and the streets were filled with crowds of murderers, rushing into the English residences, and carrying off all the valuables they could lay their hands on.

In our distant barracks we were preparing for church parade, but, as soon as the alarm reached us, we started off in haste, and, coming upon the rascals at their work of destruction, we poured into them volleys of grape and musketry, drove them from the town and pursued them in their retreat, killing great numbers. Many of them escaped to Delhi, thirty-five miles off, where three regiments of native infantry and a battery of native artillery were stationed, under Brigadier-General Graves, without a single company of British soldiers. They crowded into the city early on the following day, shouting their battle-cry, "Deen, Deen!" and cutting down every European they met, and even exceeding the atrocities of Meerut.

A few of the English officers and residents had taken refuge in the powder magazine, which was in charge of two officers and three or four subalterns, where they made a most gallant defence against the united forces of the rebels, repelling their attacks by volleys of grape. Thousands still pressed forward, applying scaling-ladders to the walls, and, just at the moment of their success, Lieutenant Willoughby, one of the officers in charge, having laid a train to the powder, gave the signal for it to be fired by Conductor Scully, and instantly the building, with hundreds of Sepoys who were crowding into it, was blown into the air.

The handful of defenders managed to escape in the confusion, carrying with them the blackened and almost lifeless body of the gallant Willoughby, who died in Meerut shortly afterwards, and leaving behind the scorched and shattered body of the noble Scully.

A few Englishmen who had attempted to hold a small fortified bastion within the Cashmere gate, called the Main-guard, were massacred by the treacherous Sepoy guard on whom they depended. Others, who had fled to the palace for protection, were murdered in the presence of the King, who was over eighty years old, his sons being also present, and thus every British resident in Delhi was slaughtered.

It is very evident that the rebels intended to clear their country of its conquerors, for I learned that when a native servant was anxious to spare a child or hide an Englishwoman, the mutineers repeated the following Persian verse:—

*"To extinguish the fire and leave a spark,*
*To kill a snake and preserve its young,*
*Is not the wisdom of men of sense."*

On returning to Meerut after chasing the mutineers, we were all ordered to remove to Dum-Dum, which is a large piece of ground enclosed by a wall, as far as I can remember about eight feet high, against which we threw up intrenchrnents and earthworks, and made loopholes for the rifles and embrasures for the guns. There were three large buildings within the enclosure, used as laboratories, and into these we put about a hundred and fifty women and children, and when all arrangements were completed the troops moved off to Delhi, leaving me with some two hundred men of all regiments, some sick and some convalescent, to mount guard; and here we remained for some months, taking turns in watching night and day, with no letters, no papers, no tobacco, and no news from outside. When the country round us was quieted down a little, some fifty or sixty of us were relieved, and, marching to Umballah, we joined a flying column, and pushed on to join the Central India Field Force at Jubbulpore, under Sir George Whitlock. Thence we made for Saugor, where the right wing of the 42nd Native Infantry had mutinied while the left wing had remained loyal, and the two wings had fought a regular pitched battle on the parade ground before we arrived, but hearing that we were only a few miles off, the right wing beat an orderly retreat towards Delhi, marching away with their colours flying.

As a precautionary measure we took the arms from the loyal left wing, but allowed them to carry their ramrods, and they marched with us through the jungle. On nearing Loghasi our advance guard came upon a large body of the enemy on a prominent hill, the sides of which were covered with dense jungle.

We did good work with our guns, and our infantry had a hard fight for the hill. After a severe struggle, in which we lost a good many men, we succeeded in driving the rebels from their position, capturing their guns, and taking one hundred and forty prisoners. The next day every one of them was hung on the trees surrounding the camp, simply hauled off the ground by ropes around their necks, and left to die and be devoured by the birds.

We pressed on again for a considerable distance, and encamped; and about eight o'clock in the evening we marched out, leaving the camp standing. We took up a position with the artillery on each flank, infantry in the centre, cavalry in the rear, and cavalry vedettes to cover the front. As night fell we threw out outlying pickets, and so remained until four the next morning, when, without sound of bugle or beat of drum, we advanced, and after proceeding about three miles, the enemy's guns opened the ball, to which we quickly replied, and soon the fighting became general.

We advanced, driving the enemy across a river, which was a shallow tributary of the Ganges, I believe. Crossing the river with an advance guard, we found, to our great surprise, that the mutineers had dug rifle-pits on a level with the river banks, which extended for more than half a mile, and from these they potted our men off, one at a time, as we waded across.

I incautiously peeped into one of these pits, and my curiosity nearly cost me my life, for inside were three Pandies, or Sepoys, who immediately opened fire on me and a chum who was just behind me. We retired a few yards, but came back and despatched the three of them with our carbines, taking their rifles, belts, and ammunition into the camp as trophies. Their commissariat supply consisted of a chatty of water, a few small bags of rice, and one or two chupatties, or native cakes.

When the column had gained the opposite bank, the infantry deployed into line, and captured a large village on our left, where they slaughtered large numbers of the rebels, all wearing Her Majesty's uniform. There were no prisoners taken, and no quarter given.

A rather strange incident occurred here. A black troop of horse artillery was ordered to the front, covered by the 12th Lancers; when in a swinging trot, without a word of command, they broke into a rapid gallop and endeavoured to join the rebels. The lead driver of No. 1 gun was immediately shot by the English officer in charge, and this checked the remainder, who were ordered to the rear, while the English troop of horse artillery, dashing to the front, came into action with a most destructive fire, being covered by the 12th Lancers. The mutineer cavalry made a move to outflank our batteries, but were checked by a most brilliant charge of the 12th Lancers, in which Sir George Wombwell's horse was shot under him.

The mutineers stood their ground well for about fifteen minutes, and then broke, and retired in the utmost confusion. It was a glorious sight to see them run. We limbered up and followed them for a considerable distance, firing at them as long as they remained in masses, until at last they became scattered in small groups all over the plain, whilst their cavalry escaped across the river, upon the banks of which, I remember, there was a large fort, which our siege-train opened fire on and knocked to pieces. We advanced up the banks of the river, and encamped for the night on the ground lately occupied by the mutineers.

We then had to bury our dead before turning in; we had two chaplains with us, one a Protestant and the other a Catholic, and they read the services over the graves which held our men. The blacks, of whom I should say there were a thousand dead on the field, were left for the jackals and vultures, which do all the scavenging in India.

Early in the morning we struck camp, and after a sharp encounter took possession of the city of Banda, and soon had the British flag once more flying over the palace, while the troops were paraded, and a royal salute fired, after which some of us were quartered in the palace.

This was the first engagement of the 3rd Madras European Regiment, now the 108th, which was raised at Bellary in November 1854 by Sir George Whitlock, and called by him his "younkers." The dash and gallantry of this young regiment could not be surpassed, and brought cheers from the old soldiers who watched their movements.

Sir George was delighted with them, and after the fight paraded them and praised them loudly. He was a most excellent officer, and a great favourite with the men. He rode a mule in the action before Banda, and it was a common sight, when on the march, to see him allow the drummer boys to ride in turns upon it while he walked by its side, for he took a fatherly interest in the young boys of the regiment.

For nearly the whole of the month following, the General and Commissioner were trying the mutineers, so that every morning before breakfast the infantry had to take part in the execution of between twenty and thirty of them, whom they hung on a large gallows in front of the palace gates. The artillery and cavalry had always enough to do to look after their horses.

The Rajah of the city got away, but we managed to capture his Prime Minister, and after standing his trial he was brought out for execution. I was close to him, and saw what a fine big fellow he was, weighing over twenty-two stone, and wearing a dress covered with gold and jewels. He was offered his liberty if he would disclose where the Rajah was hiding. He called out, "You English dog!" and spat at the officer who had charge of him, whereupon he was hoisted off his feet, and hung there writhing and kicking for ever so long.

I believe the sergeant who had charge of the hanging party obtained possession of the diamond from his turban, and the other jewels, I suppose, were not left for the birds. But we had nothing like the loot that one would expect, seeing the vast riches that were strewn about. We were unable to carry much about with us, and in consequence had to leave it for the natives who were under the command of the prize agents. Many kind promises were made by the generals, so that we all expected to live in plenty to the end of our days.

On the 8th of June 1858, we marched from Banda, for the capture of Kirwee and all its gold bricks, of which we had heard so much. We arrived at the banks of the river on the 10th, when the Rajah, Naran Roe, accompanied by his two sons and a large retinue of servants, came out and gave up his sword to our General, after which he was placed a prisoner under a European guard, and the palace was garrisoned by two companies of the 42nd Light Infantry.

The three hundred wives of the Rajah, on our approach, fled from the palace, snatching up what treasures they could find, and not stopping to pick up the valuables they dropped in their flight. We found the place strewn with an indescribable assortment of trinkets, jewels, slippers, bracelets, chains, and female finery, and on resuming our march we came upon fifty of these women hiding in a small village.

One of the Rajah's sons had shot his English tutor a day or so before we arrived. I had several talks with him while we were in charge of the palace, and found him an interesting and intelligent young man. Eventually he and his father and brother were sent to the Andaman Islands.

Most of the native troops, on our arrival marched out of the city at the opposite side, and took up a position on a high hill, posting themselves behind a breastwork of large bales of cotton, each about nine feet long.

About three in the morning we started to attack their position, and got under the hill before they were aware of our approach. We went up in three divisions, each division having two mortars, while the cavalry and artillery went round to the right to cut off their retreat. The infantry swarmed up the hill, and found the rebels preparing their breakfast. A fierce struggle ensued, and we, with the guns, had our hands full to load and fire, mowing down the men as they endeavoured to fly. The slaughter was tremendous. We took, I should say, three hundred prisoners, and then came that horrible butchery which Englishmen practised then for the first and last time -- and then, I suppose, only as a necessity; for the mutiny had to be stamped out, and I am sure we all expected to lose our lives in trying to regain possession of the country.

Our prisoners had no fear of death, and were marvellous in their immovability. We took them out into an open space and tied them together six at a time, placing them with their backs turned towards half a dozen guns, and at a little distance from them.

As we placed them in position they never moved a muscle, and some of them spat at us and called us dogs. When the word was given to fire, thirty-six of them were blown to pieces. This was repeated over and over again, and as the heaps accumulated, we drew the guns back, and continued the slaughter till the men were all destroyed.

The value of the riches found in Kirwee was beyond the power of man to imagine. Heaps of jewels and gold were found stowed away, and the gold bricks were so numerous that it took thirty bullock-waggons to remove the treasure, an Englishman and a Sepoy being placed to guard each waggon.

At a parade about this time the General said that every man who heard him, if he were spared to return to England, would be worth £500. Alas! the most fortunate of us only received £75, and that after a considerable delay, owing to a lawsuit brought by General Rose, who was in command of another column a hundred miles away, and who claimed to be entitled to half the Kirwee prize-money.

I know several old soldiers who have to keep themselves and their wives on seven shillings a week, while I have heard it said that the Government has still half a million of prize-money undistributed. I suppose I must not complain, for I am not hard pinched, although I imagine I could stand the trial of a few extra shillings a week to add to my comforts, while sitting by my own fireside, and looking back upon my twenty-one years of service.

## ALSO FROM LEONAUR
### AVAILABLE IN SOFTCOVER OR HARDCOVER WITH DUST JACKET

**EW2** EYEWITNESS TO WAR SERIES
**CAPTAIN OF THE 95th (Rifles)** by Jonathan Leach

An officer of Wellington's Sharpshooters during the Peninsular, South of France and Waterloo Campaigns of the Napoleonic Wars.

SOFTCOVER : ISBN 1-84677-001-7
HARDCOVER : ISBN 1-84677-016-5

**WF1** THE WARFARE FICTION SERIES
**NAPOLEONIC WAR STORIES**
by Sir Arthur Quiller-Couch

Tales of soldiers, spies, battles & Sieges from the Peninsular & Waterloo campaigns

SOFTCOVER : ISBN 1-84677-003-3
HARDCOVER : ISBN 1-84677-014-9

**EW1** EYEWITNESS TO WAR SERIES
**RIFLEMAN COSTELLO** by Edward Costello

The adventures of a soldier of the 95th (Rifles) in the Peninsular & Waterloo Campaigns of the Napoleonic wars.

SOFTCOVER : ISBN 1-84677-000-9
HARDCOVER : ISBN 1-84677-018-1

**MC1** THE MILITARY COMMANDERS SERIES
**JOURNALS OF ROBERT ROGERS OF THE RANGERS** by Robert Rogers

The exploits of Rogers & the Rangers in his own words during 1755-1761 in the French & Indian War.

SOFTCOVER : ISBN 1-84677-002-5
HARDCOVER : ISBN 1-84677-010-6

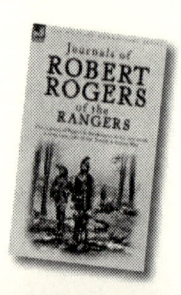

AVAILABLE ONLINE AT
## www.leonaur.com
AND OTHER GOOD BOOK STORES